HOFFMAN LAW
109 11th Ave SE
Calgary, AB T2G 1C6

Dear Judge,

Children's Letters to the Judge

Compiled by Charlotte Hardwick

Dear Judge,

ISBN 1-58747-008-X
Copyright 2002, Revised 4th Edition 2010, Pale Horse Publishing

The purchaser of this book is granted license for the individual use of this information for his or her personal use in their child custody case. All rights reserved. This material may not be published, broadcast, rewritten, or redistributed. Reproduction for distribution or resale is prohibited. Persons, companies, or entities reproducing or distributing this book in violation of this license in part or full, agree to pay the retail charge per view/use from the time of first use/view, and agree to pay any costs incurred by Pale Horse Publishing to enforce this license.

All rights reserved. No part of this work may be reproduced, stored in a retrieval system, transmitted in any form or by any means, electronic, mechanical, photocopying, recording, or otherwise, or adapted to any other medium without the prior written permission of the publisher. Brief quotations as set forth in "Fair Use" in articles or reviews are permitted and publisher requests a copy of the article or review.

This Agreement is governed by United States laws. Any dispute arising out of or with this agreement, including any question regarding its existence, validity or termination, shall be referred to and finally resolved by suit or an arbitration process approved by the Publisher. The place of suit or arbitration shall be Livingston, Polk County, Texas, USA.

Contact publisher at:
Pale Horse Publishing (936) 327-1104
http://www.palehorsepublishing.com   divorce@livingston.net

These letters are not presented in any specific order.
Enter the minds and hearts of these children at your own risk.

Children's Letters to the Judge

Preface

This book was created in an entirely different manner than any of our other books. During a continuing education class at a conference for attorneys, I spoke with a gentleman who asked to inspect a copy of the Win Your Child Custody War manual. He asked if he could keep it for a day or two. I made arrangements to pick up the manual at his office later in the week.

When I arrived at his office, his clerk informed me the judge was unavailable, and she gave me the book and a large manila envelope. I thanked her and left. Besides several good suggestions and two important case cites for the Win Your Child Custody War manual, the envelope included a stack of letters with a handwritten note that read:

"Dear Charlotte,
    I have been on the bench in family court for more than 30 years. I always worked to protect children and secure a safe happy future for them. Often I have had to work with laws with which I disagreed, attorneys I didn't like and parents I couldn't get to see past their own pain and anger. I have lost more sleep about decisions I had to make than anyone would believe.
I don't know why I saved these letters, the first one arrived the first month I was on the bench. Because they were ex parte communications and from children there was nothing I could do with them. I hope you will use them to help parents to understand what their children are going through. Children trusted me with their true feelings and I am trusting them to you. I would appreciate it if you would find a way to get these letters to the public."

(Name withheld by request)

My interest was piqued when I read the note from the judge, and I was eager to take on what I expected to be interesting, light reading. My realization of the volume, content and emotion the letters expressed was most often painfully jarring. As parents, none of us would let a stranger hurt our child the way these children have been hurt by the parents they love. Make sure that every parent who needs to hear these messages gets to read this book.

Dear Judge,

Introduction

Often parents must say "no" to children because of a court order. Other parents use the judge and the court order to erect barriers between the children and the other parent. We think the children write their letters in an attempt to fix the things that make them or the parents they love sad.

The family court system handles a staggering and growing caseload. Additionally, unlike most other litigation, the decision is never final. Often a family remains in court in one capacity or another for fifteen years. In an attempt to keep some order to the communications from individuals to the court, a procedure must be followed. Any communication arriving on a judge's desk that has not followed proper procedures, cannot be considered by the judge.

Thanks to one judge we have been provided a window into an often unexplored facet of child custody. Most of the letters were inadequately signed or not signed at all. Many of the children assumed the judge knew exactly who they were and much about what had happened throughout their case.

To install some uniformity, I inserted "Dear Judge," and after that, endeavored to only lightly edit the letters for understandability, striving to keep the original message intact.

Since the first publication of this book, we have received additional letters from other professionals. Some appear in this edition. All of the children's names have been changed.

Many of the letters we have are too dispiriting to print. But we hope the ones we have offered here will make you laugh and think.

I hope these letters mean as much to you as parents as they did to the judge and to me.

At your service,

Charlotte Hardwick

Children's Letters to the Judge

Judges are Required to Protect the Law

In order to avoid any appearance of impropriety or bias, a judge's staff may be instructed to intercept and return suspicious communications. Below is an example of what happened to a letter we sent. Our envelope was returned, unopened in a larger envelope, with this note of explanation.

The Family Court of the State of Delaware

July 10, 2008

To Whom it May Concern,

I am returning your documentation to you, as Judge Conner cannot consider **ex parte** communications from litigants and/or non-litigants of a case.

Very truly yours,

Virginia Reed
Judicial Secretary to
Judge Jay H. Conner

vr

Enclosure (documents)

The rule banning *ex parte* communications ensures that the court process is fair in that all parties have the same information as the judge who will be deciding the case.

When all parties have the same information, a party who disagrees with the information can contest its value in court.

Dear Judge,

Reviews

Fidelity to Their Content

Dear Charlotte, Just a note to let you know that my husband passed away this summer. I can't tell you how pleased he was with Dear Judge,. He was satisfied with the form his letters took and your fidelity to their content. His fervent hope was that fewer children will have to write letters because of this book. Thank you again. (Name withheld by request)

Great Contribution, 4/29/2008 -- Goldie Charm

I wasn't sure children wrote these letters until I showed this book to our school nurse. She assured me these were not the worst she had heard. For all adults who work with children.

Should Read, 4/22/2008 -- John Chancellor, teachthesoul.com

It is such a shame that the parents and their advocates often seem to forget that the children have an interest in the outcome of any divorce/custody case. From these letters it becomes obvious that in many cases the children are pawns used by one or both spouses to take out their rage toward the other.

It is very sobering reading. While I understand the hatred that can develop over a divorce, it seems inhumane for parents to take out their frustrations on the children or to put the children in the middle of a fight. It is well worth reading.

Heart-Wrenching, 12/19/2006, Sam Vaknin, "Malignant Self Love - Narcissism Revisited," Skopje, Macedonia

Children are the real casualties of divorce and custody battles. The most important figures in their lives - their parents - often regress to belligerent and narcissistic infantilism. In their anguish, some kids turn to the only reliable grown-up around: the judge.

These quivering voices of tiny shattered lives put in perspective all that we "adults" hold dear and "worth fighting for."

Children's Letters to the Judge

Given Children A Voice, 12/10/2006 -- Liane J. Leedom, M.D., ParentingtheAtRiskChild.com., CT.

Parents choose to bring a child into our world. In making this choice, parents have a solemn obligation to nurture that child and see that he discovers the plan the Almighty has for his life. During the turmoil of a divorce, parents often forget this obligation and may come to view a child as a possession rather than as a person with his own special purpose.

Dear Judge, has given a group of children the chance to remind us all that they are people not possessions. Possessions can be divided and shared. Children however, continue to need love and nurturing from those who chose to bring them into the world. Some children may also need to be protected from parents who brought them into the world to exploit rather than to nurture them.

Dear Judge, is good reading material for the waiting rooms of legal and mental health professionals. It is my hope that those who write our laws and those that interpret our laws will also read the letters. These letters are after all addressed to them.

Excellent Look Into Children's Hearts, 11/30/2006 -- Penny A. Zeller, Christian Author and Speaker

Dear Judge, takes the reader inside the lives of real children facing custody battles. Not only is this a great book for children to see that they are not alone in the difficulties of custody tug-of-wars, but it's also an excellent reference for parents and those who work with children in these types of situations. As someone who formerly worked with children in such situations, I would highly recommend this book.

Honesty, 5/16/2005 -- C. Yanda, mykidstoo.com

Out of the mouths of kids you will get honesty. This book is chock-full of how kids really feel about divorce, how they feel manipulated at times, and most importantly how much smarter they are about things than most divorced parents give them credit.

Dear Judge,

5 Star - Desperate To Be Heard -- 5/13/2005, Dr. Patricia K. Martin, Charlottesville, Virginia

This book provides an excellent overview of the various scenarios experienced by many children of divorce. As a clinical psychologist, I have heard from children many of the same sentiments revealed in this book. One common theme expressed by children whose parents are at odds about custody and visitation is that of helplessness. In ideal situations, children naturally turn to their parents when they are sad, worried or frightened. But when parents are in conflict, and children are concerned about "taking sides," hurting one parent's feelings, or making the parent angry, they cannot express themselves freely, and thereby receive words of comfort or reassurance. These letters represent their efforts to reach out to the one person they feel has control in these situations: The Judge.

I will recommend Dear Judge, to colleagues and clients. I will also urge parents who are considering divorce to read this book. I hope parents will take time to reflect on the letters, and understand that while children may appear resilient, they may quietly be harboring some of the same inner struggles described by the children in these Dear Judge letters.

5 Star - Great book! 8/15/2005 -- sb4peace, Virginia

As a mediator with 10 years of experience assisting separating parents decide custody, visitation and support issues, this book confirms very deeply and personally what I have seen and been told -- how parents' actions when separating can have a very deep impact on their children. This book should be required reading for professionals working with separating parents as well as parents who are separating and their children.

Proof Of What I Have Observed -- Kathy Clarkson, Ph.D.

It takes weeks and months to build enough trust with a child to get this kind of honestly felt comment. I had a notion these letters were out there. Thanks for presenting them in Dear Judge,.

Children's Letters to the Judge

5 Star - An Important Book, 7/31/2005 -- Katie "book worm," PA., Master's Degree in Human Organization Science and a B.A. in Psychology.

I have known many children who've felt stuck in the middle due to divorce.

This is one of those books that ALL parents can gain insights from! It is a compilation of letters written to a judge by children whose parents were in the midst of a divorce. Some of the letters will actually make you laugh, and others will make your heart hurt. But each one shares important insights into the minds and hearts of children who are dealing with these difficult issues.

This should be used as a handbook for divorcing parents - as it allows a peek into what hurts and what can heal these children who are trying to understand why, and what next...

I would highly recommend this book!

Remarkable Effect -- Richard Samson, J.D.

None of my words of experience or wisdom to parents have made the impact that Dear Judge, has. I have seen revenge motivated parents change overnight. The change in attitude has a remarkable effect on how they deal with the children, the other parent and me. Keep up the good work.

Goes a Long Way -- Elizabeth Scott Ph.D., M.S., M.A.

An innovative approach to encouraging a more child-sensitive divorce litigant. I have seen Dear Judge, go a long way towards straightening out some very damaged parent-child relationships. Would be a great addition to any pre-divorce class.

Touching, Sad, Distressing and Important, 4/14/2005 -- Reviewer: Adam Sacks Calabasas, CA

As a child of divorce, a divorced parent and an attorney I see this book is touching and sad but also very important to read. Parents doing through divorces are hurting their children for the long term in so many ways. Listen to their voices in his book, it's sad and touching. Divorce doesn't have to be this bad.

Dear Judge,

An Enlightening Compilation, 5/11/2005 -- Sherry Russell, "Reviewer/Author" Grief Management Consultant, Midwest Book Review, Vero Beach, FL

Children's hearts are so many times treated as a sub-text of divorce. They are many times the forgotten sufferers in parental conflict and the court system. This diverse collection of letters spotlights the thoughts and emotions ranging from distress to humor. They give an insight to how children become efficient little workers trying to understand ways to benefit their family, their situation and to understand a system that is confusing to most of us adults.

One of my favorites is a letter from a young fellow who has the solution to the courts' problems with children of divorce. He decides he should become a kid who lawyers other kids. After all, he points out; no one else is listening to the kids so perhaps this would work. This is truly an enlightening compilation.

The letters in <u>Dear Judge, Children's Letters to the Judge</u> are bumper stickers for your heart.

5 Stars, 5/3/05 -- Barbara Donahue, Author, "The Anti-Rules, Now That You've Got Him, How Do You Get Rid Of Him?"

This book is amazing. It empowers children to feel they can make a difference in their own lives. The letters should make everyone think before they act. They are thought provoking and heart wrenching.

Highly Recommended!, 5/5/2005 -- Sandra McLeod Humphrey, Character Education Consultant, kidscandoit.com, Minnetonka, MN

In some cases the kids seem more mature and more responsible than their parents, and one of the most important messages I gained from this book is that we must take the time to listen to our kids--really listen to them with our hearts as well as with our ears. A most revealing and insightful glimpse into the minds and hearts of our children.

Children's Letters to the Judge

5 - Star Ouch! I didn't know they saw so much., 5/12/2003 -- Helen Cornell

Great piece of work. I can see their faces and feel their hearts in these letters. I wanted more and could not have handled more at the same time. Buy this one and then try to keep your friends from walking off with it.

5 Star - Fear, Anger, Confusion, Love, Grief and Hope, 1/12/2003, -- Joanna Daneman, Top 10 Amazon Reviewer

A sad little commentary in the real voices of those who are most hurt by marriage break-ups.

An invaluable a guide to parents facing separation, divorce, shared or sole custody, or blended families, as well as being a very touching book to read. Whether a judge, lawyer, caseworker or even just a member of society watching families dissolve, this is about the most vulnerable members of our society -- children.

5 Star - Laugh and Cry, -- Paul Perry, Author of "Street People," 05/20/2002

Dear Judge, is one of those rare books that can make you laugh and cry at the same time. It's a gem, one that should be read by anyone who has been affected by divorce, which includes just about all of us. I'm passing my copy on to my granddaughter, who's getting married in a few months. The book should not only make her laugh and cry, it should also make her think."

First Amendment Privilege for Confidential Sources

The judges and other professionals that so kindly gave us these letters have been assured that we will protect the names of the children as well as their names.

The U.S. Constitution allows publishers to withhold sources of information and they are not required to indiscriminately disclose them on request.

In every other aspect, all efforts have been made to remain true to the content and spirit of each letter.

Dear Judge,

Where is that point in a journey
when people stop saying,
"You have a long way to go,"
and start saying,
"You've come a long way?"

for Joy

Children's Letters to the Judge

Table of Contents

My son Your Honor 21
Still happening 22
Justis Sistem 23
To be loyal 24
Kid's Support Group 25
None of us do 26
Forgotten me 27
Brother with dad 28
You than Santa 29
Being my dad 30
My real house 31
Bibles in school picture 32
Send mom email 33
Get a better job 34

He says later 35
She loves me 36
School all year 37
Screwed this up 38
Easier on us 39
Tell your mother 40
Stay home again 41
Don't understand 42
You were right 43
One parent at home 44
The hole summer 45
I would like a dad 46
Everything is cool 47
Who actually won? 48

Dear Judge,

Like your house 49
My ears pierced 50
Pretty good deal 51
Going on for me 52
Good dad now 53
Horrible to each other 54
Divorced too? 55
Letter back 56
Under your robe? 57
Never lets me call 58
New Nited Nations 59
It is rude 60
Can we trick dad 61
Very scary 62
Isnt zactly lying 63
Change my visitation 64
My name is Barbie 65
Really depends on me 66
Mommie cries 67
Changed our mind 68
Things in the order 69
What I want 70
Old ennuf 71
Just an accident? 72
On my side 73
In a new family 74
Just the kids 75
Ripping up the pictures 76
You there? 77
Hapie famble agn 78
In a perfect world 79
My aunt Patty 80
Not make me choose 81

Boss of the court 82
Are real sory 83
New plan 84
Afraid of the dark 85
Not good husband 86
Let me see you 87
Never had to move 88
Send no more help 89
Sted of divorcing 90
Ready to go back 91
Don't come to visit 92
I hate summer. 93
Send it to my mom 94
Far away from both 95
Really big happy family 96
Until someone wins 97
Kelly Court 98
Through 4 divorces 99
Bunch of trouble 100
Get the papers done 101
His Papa and Mema 102
Good stuff to visitation 103
All figured out 104
Want you to undivorce 105
Can't even tell mom 106
Dont forgot me 107
Restrict parents dating 108
Come yourself 109
Letting me see dad 110
Divorce my parents 111
Live where I want 112
Look up Suzi 113
I don't want to 114

Children's Letters to the Judge

Sit while I work 115
Didn't even unpack 116
I promise 117
With my siblings 118
Just get worsser 119
Is calmed down 120
Have mom come cook 121
Live with the Browns 122
Jail Clothes in kid size 123
Divorce my dad 124
Grumpy in court 125
I can spend it 126
Love me, hates him 127
Hitting each other 128
Search warrant? 129
Ever loved me 130
Move all the time 131
Cant copy his papers 132
One mom and one dad 133
Not required of you 134
No such of a thing 135
See your grades 136
Need the money 137
Isn't old enough 138
I dont care 139
Out of control 140
Dont you care 141
Hell for ternity 142
Dan lets me hang 143
Started kids court 144
Be a wrestler 145
Both say he stinks 146
Only smile 147
Pull myself out 148
Still be sweeping 149
Wants us kids to hate 150
Their own worries 151
Stinks for me 152
Made them cry 153
Can I take my cat 154
I get nervous 155
Kids lawyers club 156
This system stinks 157
Frequent flyer miles 158
You decide 159
Leave me alone 160
Doesn't hurt or feel 161
Walk home slow 162
Not allowed to talk 163
Musta done something 164
Girlfriend is naked 165
Not going back 166
Dropped us off 167
Not what I wanted 168
Really a drag 169
If you need advice 170
Need each other 171
Something about mom 172
I am sorry 173
We lied about dad 174
Having a dad before 175
Hollywood judge 176
Would like to trade 177
Better with him gone 178
Probably be unadopted 179
Both of my parents 180

Dear Judge,

Live with Dwayne 181
I should not worry 182
With my grandmother 183
Grannys fault 184
Stopped listening 185
We look fine 186
Still love her two 187
Nobody can see me 188
Trash my first letter 189
Live at my school 190
Proud of my A 191
Did I do wrong? 192
He is a slob 193
Don't live in the car 194
Hard to remember 195

Not have a divorce 196
Has a star 197
Mom is a dancer 198
Instead of protecting 199
My responsibility 200
Funeral Notice 201
To protect them 202
Cutting herself again 203
Week in Alaska 204
They don't even ask 205
What I asked for 206
Every Friday night 207
We are all back 208
Parental abduction 209
Outside this time 210

Dear Judge,

Children's Letters to the Judge

Dear Judge,

Children's Letters to the Judge

1. Dear Judge,

How are you? I am fine. I hope your weather is fine. My weather is fine.

I have some questions I would like to ask you.

When animals get a divorce do they go to you or a special animal judge like the animal doctor?

When you marry people does God let you be a Pastor for that day?

Who grades your papers? And what happens if you make a mistake?

When your Mother introduces you to people does she say this is my son Your Honor?

Your friend,

Sherri

Dear Judge,

2. **Dear Judge,**

   Its still happening. You didn't fix it yet.

   Waylon

Children's Letters to the Judge

3. Dear Judge,

My stepdad esplained the Justis Sistem to me. It does not sound right.

Trillin

Dear Judge,

4. Dear Judge,

I thought the worst moment of my life was when my mom told me she and dad were getting a divorce.

I was wrong. This is the worst. Which ever parent I am with wants me to be loyal. I can only prove my loyalty by saying I don't want to be with the other parent. The other parent is worried that I will stop loving that parent because of something the parent I am with said. Then I get dropped off or picked up and it starts all over again.

It's like sixth grade when two of my girlfriends made me crazy trying to force me to pick one of them to be my best friend.

I remember when I was sad sometimes. Now I have trouble remembering when I wasn't sad.

Yours truly,

Bailey A.

Children's Letters to the Judge

5. Dear Judge,

When they told us they were getting a divorce my whole world changed. I was so blown away I just put my feelings on hold. At home I clammed up and at school I acted like nothing was wrong.

Catrina came to school in crumpled looking clothes and was crying all day. I never really liked or talked to her before. I found her in the bathroom after school and asked her what was wrong. She told me that her dad threw her and her mom out of the house last night and they were getting a divorce. We both started crying. When I got home I called my best friend Laura who's parents were divorced two years ago. We decided to start a Kids of Divorce Support Group.

We meet after school on Thursday afternoon to talk about our feelings, what is going on at home and share ideas for handling tough situations. We have a reading list and have made our own recordings of some of the books for members who would rather listen to tapes than read.

If you deal with kids who need help we would like to recommend some books.

It's Not the End of the World, Will Dad Ever Move Back Home?, My new mom and Me, Our Family Got a Divorce, I Think Divorce Stinks, What If I Promise To Be a Better Boy?, Talking About Divorce, How to go to, Visitation Without Throwing Up, Putting It Together.

Hope this helps some other kids.

The Members of Kids of Divorce, Bakersfield

Dear Judge,

6. **Dear Judge,**

   I sure hope you know what you are doing cause none of us do.

   Jordan

Children's Letters to the Judge

7. Dear Judge,

I really need your help. My parents have forgotten me. They feed me and take me to the places I need to go. But they can only see how much they hate each other. Not how I feel.

Ya wanna know how I remember my important days? Not by how neat it was or how much fun it was but by what argument my parents had.

I work really hard and then my reward is some stupid fight. They fight over who spent what for my outfit and who has the most right to be there.

If I let either of them know I am sad, I have to hear about how it is the fault of the other one that I am going through this.

It is impossible to tell them what I think.

Yours truly,

Calrissa

Dear Judge,

8. **Dear Judge,**

   Please let my brother live with dad.

   Love,

   Amanda

Children's Letters to the Judge

9. Dear Judge,

Would I do any better writing to you than Santa?

Emily A.

Dear Judge,

10. Dear Judge,

Tell my mom if she wants to divorce my dad she can. But tell her she can't divorce him from being my dad.

Melinda K.

Children's Letters to the Judge

11. Dear Judge,

tell the home study estimater that we do not really live in the nice house she came to. we live at the crumy one. my step mother made a deel with the ladie next door and we moved there fore one day. i want you to tell her to come to my real house cause i hate my step mother that is why. cause my stomich feels upset cause she tells my real mom i am not here when she calls.

my dad said she is a ok guy but she is not. he does not like her very much eather. she play acts that she likes me but when dad is away she stops acting.

pleasee help me get to live with my mom and new sister.

thank you vere munch,

emile e.

Dear Judge,

12. Dear Judge,

    This summer we went to our bio-moms house for 6 weeks of out of state visitation. It was cool during the first week or so. Mom started asking questions about our friends and school. We told her about what we thought about the dress code, curfew and separating us into different home rooms at school because they think twins need to learn independence from each other. She said we were out of control, disrespectful of authority and needed more discipline. We tried to explain that we get good grades, follow the rules even if we don't like them and we never get in trouble. The really bad arguments with her went on for almost two weeks. It wasn't until Daddy called to see how things were going that mom finally calmed down. Daddy told mom that we were good girls, and get very good grades, act just like our friends and that we were normal. The next day she started to take more of her nerve pills and blame us for things we didn't do. Mom bought us some strange bibles and we had to study them at the kitchen table from right after breakfast until lunch time every day. It didn't go so well after that. Mom acts different from the other adults we know and doesn't have any friends. We think that means that something is wrong.

    When we I got home, we told Daddy about what had happened, how mom said that Daddy was brain washing us and that we were headed down the wrong path in life, which we are not.

    It is very uncomfortable being with her. The bible in this package is from mom. After you look at it please send it back. She will think I threw it away if I don't have it the next time. Mom wants to see our bibles in our school pictures so she knows we are studying each day.

    We don't want to go back to her house anymore, but it is your court law for us to go. Can you have her come here for visitation?

Tracy and Lacy A.

Children's Letters to the Judge

13. Dear Judge,

I live with my dad and that's cool. My dad says he is getting me a computer for my birthday and that's cool.

At one visit my mom gave me her work email and that's how it got started. I have been sending e-mail back and forth to my mom for about a year using my best friend's computer and that's cool.

The problem is that I have never told my dad that my mom and I email each other almost every day and that's not cool. My dad is a real solid guy and he is really going to be disappointed when he finds out that I have been doing something behind his back.

I would like to be able to send mom email from home and have dad know about it. I would like some advice about this.

Respectfully,

Megan P.

Dear Judge,

14. Dear Judge,

In Sunday School they told us that God does not want people to get divorced. They said people get divorced with a judge so they can marry new people. How about if you tell people to stay married so they do not have to marry again. We can find you a better job.

In Christs Name,

Sterling B.

Children's Letters to the Judge

15. Dear Judge,

when i ask my dad if i can call my mom he says later. when i ask later he gets sad and says am i not hapy here. i am happy with him i just want to talk to my mom

when i get home my mom ask me why i did not call her. i told her that it makes dad sad when i want to call her. she says it makes her sad when i dont not call her. mom said if i love her i should call her. mom said you said i could call my mom or my dad when ever i want to.

i want to call my mom but i do not want to make my dad sad.

Lacy N.

Dear Judge,

16. Dear Judge,

Please tell my mom not to worry. I know the truth and I know she loves me.

April

Children's Letters to the Judge

17. Dear Judge,

My teacher said the guys who make the laws decid if we can come to school all year long. I love school because there is no grownups yelling and hitting. If you tell the guys who make the laws to get rid of sumer vacation it would be real good. I will tell the kids it is good and then every thing will be real good.

I will be your frend forever,

Kyle G.

18. Dear Judge,

Boy, you guys really screwed this up.

C.P.

Children's Letters to the Judge

19. Dear Judge,

Thank you for the decision you made. At first I didn't think it was going to work out.

I think my parents started to put up with each other because your court order told them they had to and just how they had to do it.

Then I think they kept it up because neither of them wanted to look bad to their friends and at church.

Now I think they get along to make things easier on us. And it is easier.

Thanks again,

Kyle P.

Dear Judge,

20. Dear Judge,

If I was you I would not tell no one what I do all day. I think you should specially not tell your mother cause she would be very disapointed in you. If you want to not make your mother sad you should try harder. If you do a better job you wont make my mom sad no more to.

You can tell when you are doing better because you get smile faces on your papers.

Iona

Children's Letters to the Judge

21. Dear Judge,

Last sumner I broke my leg the day before I was spose to go on a airplain to visit my dad. The docter sayd I could go in a week but my dad didnot have fundable tickets and did not have money for new tickets so I did not have to go.

At Christmas visit I had the flu too much and didnot have to go again.

If I break something again can I stay home this sumner again?

Dallas S.

22. Dear Judge,

I don't understand. I don't think I will ever understand.

Armand R.

Children's Letters to the Judge

23. Dear Judge,

You were right. We are going to be alright.

Bethany

Dear Judge,

24. Dear Judge,

In my class we have more kids with one parent at home than we have kids with two parents at home. We have to do a report on how people think about single parents and the affect on kids. I have decided to make my report about how movies show kids dealing with it.

These are the movies I found.

The Champ 1931
The Women 1939
Mr. Skeffington 1944
Child of Divorce 1946
Trouble Along the Way 1953
Doubtfire 1993
A Thousand Clowns 1965
Petulia 1968
Paper Moon 1973
Alice Doesn't Live Here Anymore 1974
Kramer v. Kramer 1979
Author! Author! 1982
E.T. 1982
Irreconcilable Differences 1984
The Good Mother 1988
Ghost Dad 1990
Curly Sue 1991
Mermaids 1990
My Girl 1991
Radio Flyer 1992
The Sandlot 1993
The Good Son 1993
The Parent Trap 1961
Mrs. Man Without a Face 1993
Jack the Bear 1994
Simple Twist of Fate 1994
Bye Bye Love 1995
Man of the House 1995
Three Wishes 1995
Losing Isaiah 1995
Jack and Sarah 1995
Hollow Reed 1996
Liar Liar 1997
The Stepmother 1998
A Cool, Dry Place 1998
Big Daddy 1999

I would appreciate it if you would add any titles you know about that I did not list. I am finding and watching these movies and writing a paragraph about what they say on my subject. My life is most like 'Bye Bye Love'.

Yours truly,

Charity S.

Children's Letters to the Judge

25. Dear Judge,

My dad used to mak me come for the hole sumer. He was workin all the tim and I had to be with the old lady up stairs. I did say I did not want to go for the hole sumer a bunch of times.

This year he did not send me any ticket. Mom said I naged him to not go and now I nag him to go. Only I feel real sorry cus I miss him. I still want to be his son. He said he only has enuf for the child suport and so he will mayb see me Thanksgivin.

Can I take back the first nag and go to my dad?

Yours Truley,

Richard R.

Dear Judge,

26. Dear Judge,

The television said half of the people who get married are getting divorced. I think about half of those people are dads.

Some of them dads must still be good. My mom has never been married and I would like a dad.

Could you put this picture of me and my mom on the front of your desk in the court. If a good dad that is getting kicked out of his family needs a new one, please make sure he sees our picture. If a bad dad sees our picture and asks about us tell him we are not home.

I am pretty and a good girl. My mom is pretty and a good mom. We have a house and will get a dog if you think it will help.

Thank you,

Trish P.

Children's Letters to the Judge

27. Dear Judge,

Everything is cool. Don't worry about us anymore. My dad changed from the Huntsville to the Houston Fire Department and gets more pay with almost the same job. The nights he is away I stay with the Abromivits family next door.

I learned to make the checks out for the bills my dad stacks in a pile. He autographs them and sends them out. Mrs. Abromivits taught me to make and cook a menu for the week and make a shopping list for dad from that.

I really want to stay here with my dad. I love my grandparents but don't want to live with them. They never wanted my mom to marry my dad so they don't think much of him. He is a really good man and a great dad.

We have been without mom for almost a year. We both miss her very much and need each other to keep mom alive in our hearts. My grades are good and I don't miss any school. I will be thirteen in four months and know what I want.

My grandparents only come to visit at Christmas and we would like them to come just like they always do. But, I don't want to live with people I only see once a year my whole life.

Sincerely yours,

Abra Z.

28. Dear Judge,

So who actually won?

Brandi

Children's Letters to the Judge

29. Dear Judge,

I asked Dad what you were before you were a judge and he said a lawyer. I told my Dad that lawyers must be baby judges and he laughed with me.

I really like your house. I come with my Dad to file some papers. We ate snacks out of the machine and went to the bathroom and got a drink.

I did not see your kitchen or bedroom. We have three bedrooms. You must have about a milion since you have so many people in your family.

You need some swings in your yard.

Your friend,

Faith L.

Dear Judge,

30. Dear Judge,

Mom said I can get my ears pierced if I stop being a pill about visitation. I really want my ears pierced but I hate going to visit my dad and step mother.

How old do I have to be to get to decide if I go to visitation or not? All the girls at my lunch table have their ears pierced and if I have to wait until I am 14 that will be too long.

Anitra G.

Children's Letters to the Judge

31. Dear Judge,

This is a pretty good deal. My mom and dad are working real hard to show Miss. Lee who is better for me to live with. I hope she takes a long time to decide.

When she talked to me I told Miss Lee I was having a good time. She laughed with me. She said I might be the only real grown up in this.

I thought about it and I think you should have Miss Lee give you a report card about my parents just like I get a report card from school.

In a couple of years you could decide after you look at the report cards. If you don't think they have made enough progress you could just wait to choose.

Sincerely,

Ronnie M.

32. Dear Judge,

I dont think what is going on for me is the same as what is going on for my parents.

I dont know who is right. I dont not care who is right.

Clare C.

Children's Letters to the Judge

33. Dear Judge,

I need you to help me. My dad is trying to be a good dad now. He used to stink at it but he is trying reel hard.

My mom says he is a liar and a cheat and you can never trust him. But he is not doing any of that stuff now.

My mom does stuff to make it so my dad messes up. She thinks I don't know it but I do. Dad knows it to but he does not say nothing.

My dad is getting good at finding out where I will be and has been showing up on his own. I was the only guy who did not have a dad before. Please make it easier for my mom so she won't be so mad.

Yours very truly,

Brian B.

Dear Judge,

34. Dear Judge,

Please order my parents to stop acting horrible to each other. They call each other names and yell when they get close. They spend their time with me telling me how bad each other is.

I can't even have my friends over because my parents are so bad. I hate going home and my stomach hurts all the time. I have tried to talk to them but no one listens to me.

Please help as soon as you can.

Connie C.

Children's Letters to the Judge

35. Dear Judge,

When our parents get their divorce do we have to get a divorce too? Sharon and me don't want to divorce our parents. We just want them to get a divorce so they could be friends again. They said they were friends for a long time before they got married. We think if they get a divorce they could be friends and be nice to each other again.

Grandma says for us children to ignore our parents and keep being good and happy children. It is hard but grandma let's us call her when we are worried and she tells us what to do. Dad and mom even listen to grandma sometimes.

So divorce mom and dad, but not the rest of us. We are going to do what grandma says until mom and dad feel better.

Thank you for reading our letter.

Buddy and Sharon E.

Dear Judge,

36. Dear Judge,

When I didnt get a letter back from you I thought you werent going to help me. But as you know everything has worked out.
I just wanted to say Thank You.

Merry Christmas,

Leanna J.

Children's Letters to the Judge

37. Dear Judge,

For about 4 years I have been very interested in becoming a judge. I am 10 now but am growing up real fast.

I have some questions before I sign up. Do judges have homework? Do the same kind of judges who marry people divorce people? What do you have on under your robe? I see delivery men and nurses in their work clothes in the supermarket. I don't never see any judges in their robes. Where do judges go to buy their groceries?

If I have to use my own computer for work can I keep the games in it so I have something to do between the court cases? Do judges get to stay up after 8:30 at night? If I don't like the sound that my gavel makes can I use a bell or horn instead?

Hope to be working with you soon.

Michael M. III

Dear Judge,

38. Dear Judge,

My mom never lets me call my dad when I am at visitation with her.
So my dad got me a cell phone. How cool is that!
So if she takes it away do I still have to go to visitation? I don't think I should have to.

Chad L.

Children's Letters to the Judge

39. Dear Judge,

Would you pleas have the New Nited Nations make it peace at my hous. We lerned about them at school today. I asked my Dad if he thinks it would help us. He said he did not think they stopped the fiting any place he new about.

If they stop fiting at my house they would be able to do it every wher. We will be on their comercial on tv and tell people what a good job they do.

My hous would be a good place to start cause it is close and they could go home at the nite time.

Dad said may be if they sent in peace kepers it would help but I think you have to have some peace to kep first and we don't have any.

Love,

Dawn

Dear Judge,

40. Dear Judge,

It is rude that you didn't answer my letters. I really needed your help. You have your job because you are supposed to be wiser that the other grown-ups. I guess wiser doesn't mean kinder.

I am not going to give you my name this time. I am sure you will not be able to figure out who I am. My Grandmother says 'How you do anything is how you do everything.' So I am sure you don't remember my name.

I will never forget your name.

Children's Letters to the Judge

41. Dear Judge,

Cathy Stanley is the smartest girl in our class. She spent the summer with her grandmother in Wisconsin. She says my mom can trick dad into moving back home with us and make him love us again. Cathy Stanley said she is sure it will work cause it even worked for some bad lady on the soap opera.

My mom is a good lady. I just want to know if it is legal to trick dad to get him to come home. I am asking because last summer Cathy Stanley and I got in trouble for trying to take the air bag out of her mothers car. Cathy's mother said it was anainst the law to take the air bag out of a car. So I don't want to get grounded.

We are waiting for your answer. If you say no we won't trick my dad. If you say yes Cathy Stanley has a plan all ready to go.

Sharon P.

Dear Judge,

42. Dear Judge,

When ever I go for visitation it is very scary. The first night always feels like I have never been there before. I don't like it.

Trudy C.

Children's Letters to the Judge

43. Dear Judge,

i thot my dad was cool cauze he could make every one believe him. even the cops is fooled. we always laf at them. dad said it isnt zactly lying cauze they dont have no busnes in our stuff any way. the first time i seen him tell a lie i thot he just made a mistak but later we was laughing cuse the guy was a jerk. we all told the childrns servs lady that dad didnt hit mike when he was bad. so mom got in trouble for call them on us. i dont think dad is so cool now caus he is hitting us and the childrns servs lady wont come back. mike is reel hurt som times. i think my dad lies to me now to.

Steven P.

Dear Judge,

44. Dear Judge,

Pleases change my visitation from one night and every other weekend with my mom. Some weeks I am in a different place to sleep every other night.

I need to spend more time with my mom. I would like you to change my visitation to the same as Lacy has with her parents.

All day Sunday, Monday, Tuesday and half a day Wednesday with mom.

Half a day Wednesday, all day Thursday, Friday and Saturday with dad.

This will work for school and summertime and give me lots of time with them both and they will be able to have a life to.

Please start this as soon as possible.

Sincerely,

Destiny S.

Children's Letters to the Judge

45. Dear Judge,

Now when I go to the dinner table my name is Barbie. I keep my face in a nice smile and sit up like a lady.

Barbie just thinks about her pretty clothes and all the fun things she is going to do when she grows up.

Barbie never gets a nervous tumy and has to go to the bathroom fast. She never starts crying or pukes.

Barbie is polite and everyone loves her. I don't have to be Barbie at the morning cause its just Mom and me and it is real nice.

Me and Logan figured out for me to be Barbie one day and it works very good.

Your friend,

Reanna

Dear Judge,

46. Dear Judge,

I think we need some help. My mom and dad got a divorce and I live with my dad. When mom was here I was the kid of the family. Now my dad says I am the little lady of the house.

Dad has Miss Hawthorn sit me down to plan our meal menus for the week. I have to eat with the business people who come to our house. Dad says he won't ever get married again because he has me.

My dad says he really depends on me. I liked it better when I was the kid of the family. I don't understand what everyone expects me to do now. I am not ready. I am making too many mistakes.

Sincerely,

Clarice B.

Children's Letters to the Judge

47. Dear Judge,

Please tell my Dad to come home.

My mommie cries all the time and it scares me. I dont know if we are going to be alright if he doesnt come home soon.

Tell him I love him and I will be a very good girl.

Emily L.

48. Dear Judge,

We changed our mind.

Children's Letters to the Judge

49. Dear Judge,

Please send me the form to get some important things in the court order that you forgot. Whenever my mom or my dad don't want to do something the other one wants, they say, the court order doesn't say they have to.

I have started a list but my mom said that things have to be done right on the papers for the court. I called the court and the lady clerk said everything has to have the correct form to be looked at by the court.

If you will send me the right form I will fill it out with just as nice handwriting as this letter is. If it has to be done on a computer I can use one at my school.

I look forward to your letter.

Dawson W.

50. Dear Judge,

My dad said I could tell you what I want and you will let me have it.
I would like to live with my dad.
I would like a new dress for easter.
I would like soxes with rufels.
I would like shoes with bows.

Your friend,

Justina

Children's Letters to the Judge

51. Dear Judge,

Mom says I will be old ennuf to decid where I want to live when I come to her next sumer. I would like to stay living with my dad and my stepmom.

My dad goes to work after we have sereal in the morning so my stepmom waits for the bus with me. We look at natur and talk til the bus comes. She is the room mom at school and takes me to panio. My stepmom waits when my bus comes home and we cook diner. I mostly do salad and desert and set the tabl. My dad tells about his day and we eat and do home work and clean up and play yatzee.

The big kids dont live with my real mom any mor but she has a baby. My real mom works at 2 placs. We stay at the baby siter who gives us good food and cartoon tv. Some times I am aslep when mom comes. We don't have cartoon tv at my dads. I like cartoon tv.

Could you tell my real mom that you think I can not decid where to live and just stay this way.

Gillian H.

Dear Judge,

52. Dear Judge,

Did you mean for this to happen to me or was it just an accdent?

Bye,

Jeffrey J.

Children's Letters to the Judge

53. Dear Judge,

Thank you for appointing Mr.Jefferies to help me. When my mom said that you were appointing a GAL to me I thought it would be a girl.

It really helps to have someone on my side. He talked to my mom and dad and now they don't say so much bad things about each other to me.

Mr. Jefferies told me that when parents see that they are accidently hurting their children they will stop. He was right. Mr. Jefferies even set it up so I could talk to the school counselor when ever I want to.

We are getting ready for Mr. Jefferies to spend the day with me at my moms house and a different day at my dads house and see my rooms. My parents live close to each other and if I can see them both each day I don't care where I live.

Your friend,

Devon F.

Dear Judge,

54. Dear Judge,

I think my mom and dad are fighting because of me. Could you put me in a new family so my mom and dad can be happy again.

Sandy S.

Children's Letters to the Judge

55. Dear Judge,

My mom and dad got a divorce so they could marry new people.

Now I have brothers and sisters and half sisters and half brothers and step sisters and step brothers.

Is there some special word that could just mean we are all just the kids?

Except for one boy I like all the kids.

Sincerely,

Amanda N.

Dear Judge,

56. Dear Judge,

My step mom keeps ripping up the pictures I get of my mom.

Could you send her a letter and tell her she is not allowed to do that?

Tell her in the letter that I did not ask you to do it you just are going to send this letter to all the step moms.

Sinserely,

Davida P.

Children's Letters to the Judge

57. Dear Judge,

Are you there?

Douglas

Dear Judge,

58. Dear Judge,

plez com to my hows an talk to my parnts
we will all get drest nice an wrk hard to be good
i wont a hapie famble agn

yur frnd

Jamie L.

Children's Letters to the Judge

59. Dear Judge,

In a perfect world my parents wouldn't be divorced.

In a perfect world my parents could forget themselves and think about me sometimes.

In a perfect world I could share my happy thoughts with all the people I love.

In a perfect world I could have the people that are important to me at the events that are important to me.

In a perfect world you wouldn't have become the real parent in our family to make my parents act like adults.

In a perfect world I could talk to my parents instead of writing to you.

In hopes for a perfect world,

Natasha N.

Dear Judge,

60. Dear Judge,

My mom and dad want my sister and me to stay with my aunt Patty for the summer so they can try to stop their divorce.

I would like them to work things out but I dont want to stay with my aunt Patty. At Christmas I stole a bottle of her perfume and have not been able to look at her or talk to her since then.

She had a son named Marvin that tried to rob a store and shot the owner. He got arrested and went to jail. Aunt Patty said she cant bide a thief and will never talk to Marvin again.

Nobody but you and me know I did it and every time they talk about the summer I start to cry. I am really scared that no one in the family will love me any more if they find out I steal. If I go to my aunt's she will see what I did. If I dont go my parents will get a divorce for sure. I wish I could die.

Please help me,

Deana L.

Children's Letters to the Judge

61. Dear Judge,

Please dont not make me choose.

William

Dear Judge,

62. Dear Judge,

You are lucky to be the boss of the court. I don't even get to be the boss of my bedroom because I have to share it with my big brother Lewis.

When he is meen to me I call him old stinke head so he can not here me.

If you can think of a way for me to be the boss of my room pleas send me a letter.

Sincerly,

Raymond O.

Don't tell Lewis I sent this letter.

Children's Letters to the Judge

63. Dear Judge,

My mom and dad are real sorry they bothered you with our divorce.

They are both tired of giving all their money to the lawyers.

I think they can work things out now. So you can take our names off your list.

We think you did a good job but you don't know us very good.

Eugene E.

Dear Judge,

64. Dear Judge,

My mom calls me every week and tells me about the great things we are going to do when I come for visit.

When I get to her house we dont do much and there are a bunch of reasons why we cant do the things she said. I spend most of my time with the baby sitter.

After summer visit she starts telling me about Christmas and what I am going to get. That doesnt realy work out.

When I get home and tell my dad and he gets mad at my mom cause I feel so bad. I dont want my dad to get mad at mom but I need to tell him how I feel.

Dad and I decided that mom is doing the best she can. We decided that he wont get mad at her any more and I wont let my feelings be hurt. From now on when mom cant take me where she said, I am not supposed to be sad.

When I get home dad will do those things with me.

I think you should tell other kids about this plan.

Buddy M.

Children's Letters to the Judge

65. Dear Judge,

Ever since the divorce started I am afraid of the dark. Could you please put night lights in the ending court order?

Thank you,

Patty E.

Dear Judge,

66. Dear Judge,

My father was a not good husband. My mother is very mad at him. He does not ever do things the right way. He does not understand what is important and he does not take his responsibilities.

I am not supposed to like him because of all that things. I do love my dad and I like to be with him. He does the things he does with me the right way and does his responsibilities with me.

When my mother is mad at me she says I am just like my dad. That makes me feel ugly.

Your friend,

Case H.

Children's Letters to the Judge

67. Dear Judge,

Pleas tell me if you are reel. Can you let me see you? Try to let my frend Lyle see you to. He probly doesnt think you are reel ethr. I am hafing a hard tim conteroling my tempr. I ned a magic powdr to bee good.

Your beast pal,

McKenzie D.

Dear Judge,

68. Dear Judge,

I hate my new school. I dont have any friends. I wish I never had to move and start at a new school again.

Your friend,

Torie

Children's Letters to the Judge

69. Dear Judge,

Please don't send no more help cause we have more than we need.

At my school I see the student counselor on two days after lunch.

My mom and dad have been going to divorce counseling three nights every week.

Our church is giving us divorce support classes.

Since dad got his own apartment he and mom have to work more to pay bills so I spend more time with my grandparents. All my grandparents are trying to help us and they want me to talk to them about my feelings when ever they take care of me. I don't have anything else to say. I don't even know what they want me to say.

I would like to go somewhere where someone doesn't know what is going on at home. I would like to be just a kid again for awhile.

Thank you,

Clark C.

70. Dear Judge,

Sted of divorcing the families you have now and marrying the new ones why dont you just keep the ones you got now?

Viki K.

Children's Letters to the Judge

71. Dear Judge,

I am ready to go back to my mother's house. I really made a big mistake and I want you to put the old custody order back.

It is not the same living with my dad as it was visiting him. I have been visiting him for eight years every other weekend and holidays and summers. I could do anything I wanted and we always had a good time going places and doing things. When I would tell him about the things mom made me do he would be angry with me at her. He even tried to get her to do things different.

I have more responsibilities and chores here and he is worse than mom about my clothes and friends. He doesn't buy me everything now and all the sudden we got rules. Lots of rules.

I tried to talk to mom about moving home but she said that neither she nor dad were interested in changing anything back. When I tell her the things dad does she doesn't even get mad or talk to him. She said this is probably good for all of us.

I don't like it here one bit and I don't think its good for me and I want you to change it back right now. I have my things ready to go as soon as we get the letter from you.

Please take care if this first thing in the morning.

Thank you,

Francine B.

Dear Judge,

72. Dear Judge,

My grandma and grandpa don't come to visit me any more. Mommy said they don't love me any more. Is that really.

Rita

Children's Letters to the Judge

73. Dear Judge,

I hate summer. All my friends get to go to camp an do great stuff. I have to go to summer visit. I hate to fly on the airplane and I hate to spend all day with the little kids.

My mom doesn't have no time off from her jobs. She drops us off at 7 o clock at the morning and doesn't pick us up till 9 o clock at the night. When she gets a day off she doesn't have no money to do something.

None of the things she promise ever happen. I just want to stay back home with my friends and visit mom for the time she has a vacation and could spend time with me.

Please see what you can do.

Luke J.

Dear Judge,

74. Dear Judge,

Miss Geneva watches me after school so she is helping me mail this to you.

Inside you will find $37.00 that I have taken a long time to save at her house.

Please send it to my mom and baby sister. My dad and I don't have enough money to send the child support and I don't want my dad to go to jail.

Best wishes,

Brian D.

Children's Letters to the Judge

75. Dear Judge,

Please send me the definition of Best Interest of the Child. My parents have been divorced for four years now and what I want doesn't seem to matter. I don't know how to fix it but I only have one parent or the other at important events. There is always a huge fight about which of them invested the most time in the activity or organization putting on the event. That seems to be the most important part of the question. It doesn't matter if it is an honors award, sports event, recital, church activity or school open house. I have tried to tell them that these are my events and I need both my parents to attend. They say they can't stand to be any place near each other. It reminds me that if I show any traits of, or interests encouraged by the absent parent I will cause the parent with me to get angry.

If there is something I want to take part in, I have to make sure everyone has the information and then back off. It causes a whole new fight that is usually not resolved until the deadline or registration is almost closed. They both say they love me. The truth is, neither of them spend the time with me they did before the divorce. I am just something they use to hurt each other. I don't think either of them has really heard anything I have said since they split.

When I graduate in two years, I am planning to get as far away from both of them as I can. What they will use to hurt each other with then? This makes me so tired. Even when I do good I don't feel good.

Sincerely,

Carolyn

76. Dear Judge,

Well you were right. When you talked to me in your office you said it would work out someday.

My mom and her boyfriend. My dad and his new wife. All their kids and all us kids went to eat at Golden Coral for lunch today.

It was just like a really big happy family. We had to put tables together and everything.

I wish I had believed you. Because if I had really believed you then this last three years would have been a lot better.

Thank you,

Leslie S.

Children's Letters to the Judge

77. Dear Judge,

My mom and dad fight about everything. Mom says you can never rely on him for anything and dad says she is a control freak.

When mom finally says dad can pick us up for visit he doesn't want to look at her. So dad sits out in his car and honks the horn. Mom says he has to come to the door and won't let us go out to the car.

Sometimes it takes almost an hour before one of them gives in. Jake and I have to sit on the couch until someone wins. We hate it.

Samantha N.

Dear Judge,

78. Dear Judge,

Can a big sister make her own court when the real mom is at work?

If Kelly is on the phone with her boyfriend and she says we are making too much noise or we start playing to ruff or fighting or someone gets hurt and Kelly is in charge she makes us do Kelly Court.

We have to get enough kitchen and dining room chairs for everyone except Kelly who gets dad's reading chair and she puts the TV tray in front of it.

Everybody chooses what side they are on and we sit down. Kelly hammers the TV tray with the ice cream scoop and tells us who can talk first. Then she lets the next guy talk, then she decides.

If you lose you have to clean her room or do her chores. If you don't she will put you in the corner for a long time. If you don't go in the corner she will pick you up and put you in the corner.

We told mom what Kelly was doing and mom said it was OK cause before she put Kelly in charge we would call her at work 15 times a day. Kelly said it was in the law to have Kelly Court cause she saw Judge Judy on television.

If we have to do Kelly Court till Kelly is the same old as Judge Judy we will die. It will be better if you send Kelly a letter to tell her she has to go to judge school first and then be a judge.

Yours truly,
Adam
Alan
Joshua

Children's Letters to the Judge

79. Dear Judge,

I have been through 4 divorces with my mom and my dad isn't much better at choosing wives. Actually they have both made good job at finding people who I like and that like me. Right now they are talking about getting back together.

What I have figured out is that everyone is really paying attention to the grown-ups. It would help if you would tell the kids that they have to pay attention to their own lives. They can't fix things for their parents and they can't forget to keep taking care of their own stuff while this stuff is going on.

Tell kids tell the people in your family that you love them, take care of your stuff, stay in touch with your friends, keep up your grades, take care of your pets, be as self reliant as you can, stay in your clubs, sports and hobbies, watch out for your enemies, keep going to church, and most of all take care of yourself. Tell kids to leave the room is if someone is saying bad things about someone you love. Tell kids to believe people who tell them everything will work out. Tell kids to decide to be happy.

Tell kids that they shouldn't let their parents make them choose sides or try to make them carry messages back and forth. Tell kids not to make promises they are not comfortable about making. Tell kids that they are still good if they look like their mom or act like their dad. Tell kids when it is all over things are going to be however they are going to be.

Thank you for reading my letter. If you have a question send me a letter.

Sincerely,

Ramona A.

Dear Judge,

80. Dear Judge,

I am in a bunch of trouble at school. I haven't been doing my homework. We are having a bunch of trouble at my house.

When I get home I have to go to the neighbor. If my dad comes to get me Mrs. Ule has to say I am not here.

When my mom comes we go home. Sometimes my dad comes and they yell and fight. Sometimes we hide in the house and don't open the door. Last night we climbed out the window and ran down the street to my aunt's house.

Mom thinks dad will hurt us.

Please can you help us.

Yours truly,

Marlene R.

Children's Letters to the Judge

81. Dear Judge,

My mom wants the house, the suburban, and my sister and me.

My dad wants the hunting lease, the boat, the truck and the cabin.

My sister wants the playhouse in the back yard and the cat.

I want the trampoline, the go cart and the dog.

That's pretty much everything. Could you get the papers done so we dont have to listen to any more arguments?

In Jesus,

Dan E.

Dear Judge,

82. Dear Judge,

I am writing this letter for my friend Bernard cause he cant write good yet.

Bernard is living with his Papa and Mema since he was a baby and now he is 7. His Papa got some food stamps to help with the groceries last year.

The food stamp people found Bernards mom and are making her give money for Bernards food stamps.

So Bernards mom wants Bernard to come and live with her so she dont have to pay the money.

Bernard wants to stay here. We would like you to fix it so he can stay. Papa and Mema said they will give back the money and the food stamps.

Yours truly,

Bernard and Carlo

Children's Letters to the Judge

83. Dear Judge,

I am not taking any of my good stuff to visitation. The more I love something the worser they treat it.

Mitchell

Dear Judge,

84. Dear Judge,

I have this all figured out and things are much easier.
If you explain this to the other kids it will help them.
Divorce is not the end of the world.
Divorce is the end of one way a family lives.
Divorce happens, children don't cause it, and can't fix it.
Divorce is the change to a different way a family lives.
Divorce does not stop your parents from loving you.
Divorce does not stop you from loving both of your parents.
Divorce is hard at first.
Divorce will get easier.
Divorce is a time when you should talk about your feelings.
Divorce does not make you responsible for your parents.
Divorce does not make you responsible for their happiness.
Divorce is hard on everyone.
Divorce can help everyone in the family be a better person.
Divorce is something you can survive.

Very truly yours,

Kimberly J.

Children's Letters to the Judge

85. Dear Judge,

I want you to undivorce my mom and dad. It is just not working out for me.

Sincerely,

Debbie B.

86. Dear Judge,

I really need some help. When I spend the weekends with my dad we always have a great time. Sometimes we do big stuff that costs a lot of money and sometimes we just fish, work on a car or hang out together.

When dad drops me off at my mom's, in front of him, she always asks if I had a good time. If I say, yes or we had a great time she gets mad and stays that for a bunch of days. So I have to just say, It was ok.

If my dad hears me say that it was just ok he looks hurt. I asked mom why she gets mad. She said it's because dad only does this stuff with me to make her look bad and try to get custody of me because she can't afford to compete.

Dad says he isn't trying to change custody because his job will never let him be home with me as much as mom can be. Dad and I both think I am in the best place I can be except for mom's attitude.

I can't even tell mom when I am looking forward to my time with dad. I love my mom and want to be able to love my dad without feeling guilty. What can I do.

Sincerely yours,

Richard G.

Children's Letters to the Judge

87. Dear Judge,

Please dont forgot me.

Mimi S.

Dear Judge,

88. Dear Judge,

This is bogus. You should restrict parents from dating for a year after a divorce. My mother can't handle it. She pawned me off on a Big Sisters lady rather than spend time with me. None of us ever got to do anything that had anything to do with sports or after school or church.

Then mom enrolled Danny in Karate lessons. He only go to take them for a month because mom started having the instructor spend the night. When he stopped coming over mom stopped taking Danny to lessons.

Mom said dating after a divorce is normal. On most her dates the guys just come over to our house. After they send us to bed the guys stay with mom in her room. That is not a date. Mom had me when she was still in high school. I think she wants to make up for her teen years now. Except that we need at least one parent. I can't take care of three little kids.

Mom won't do what you tell her to do unless you check up on her. She will want to know why you are doing this. Tell her the neighbors were complaining again.

Very truly yours,

Candice

Children's Letters to the Judge

89. Dear Judge,

Don't send someone else to our house. You should come yourself. It is your responsibility to decide so you should not have some else do your homework. Then you will know it was done right.

Melissa

Dear Judge,

90. Dear Judge,

Thank you for letting me see my dad. I like the visiting center. The ladies are nice.

My mom is telling the ladies that visiting my dad makes my stomach hurt but it doesnt. The ride to the visitation center with my mom makes my stomach hurt.

My mom tells me to be good and have a nice visit in front of the ladies but she gets real mad at me if I do.

The ladies at the visiting center used to tell my mom I had a good time. They could see she would get mad. Now they just tell my mom that I was a good girl.

Me and dad like the center so if you will keep things this way it will be good.

Have a nice day.

Loretta W.

Children's Letters to the Judge

91. Dear Judge,

I want to divorce my parents. Since they got a divorce I do not like either one of them. I do not have any money and the lawyer I talked to downtown said there wasn't anything I could do unless they were beating me. It's not my outside that hurts. It is my heart.

They used to love each other and now they hate each other. They say they love me. I think its just a matter of time before they hate me too.

Please see what you can do for me.

Wendy C.

Dear Judge,

92. Dear Judge,

    I am twelve years old and should be able to live where I want to. I would like to live at both my parents houses. They live seven blocks apart and I would like to come and go from their houses when ever I want.

    My mom is really nice and takes good care of me. But when she is at work and my dad is off work I would like to be able to spend time with him. My mom says I can't because your court order says that I can only go to his house two weekends a month and Wednesday night. Lots of times I am alone at my house for two hours after school and dad is alone at his. I have tried to get my parents to talk about this but they can't speak to each other with out a lot of old problems popping up.

    Could you please change the court order.

Thank you,

Teresa Ann T.

Children's Letters to the Judge

93. Dear Judge,

Can you tell if somebody is a good mom just by looking at her face. My dad is going out with a pretty lady and she acts like a mom. I dont know if she really is a good mom cause I just keep thinking about her pretty face.

Could you look up Suzi in your computer and let me know.

Yours truly,

Shane M.

Dear Judge,

94. Dear Judge,

- I don't want to carry any stupid messages back and forth.
- I don't want to pick a side.
- I don't want to hear any more bad things.
- I don't want to talk to any more child cycloigsts.
- I don't want to answer questions about the other house.
- I don't want to have to lie.
- I don't want to tell what the other one is saying.
- I don't want to have to say I like here better than there.
- I don't want a new dad or mom.
- I don't want to move.
- I don't want to keep any more secrets.
- I don't want to compare presents to the presents I get.
- I don't want to listen to any more arguments.
- I don't want to make excuses for my parents bad behavior.
- I don't want to lie to keep everyone happy.
- I don't want to always need my stuff that is at the other house.
- I don't want to explain why my parents act the way they do.
- I don't want to talk about it.
- I don't want to feel guilt because I love them both.

Malachi O.

Children's Letters to the Judge

95. Dear Judge,

I dont want to work as hard on my feet as my mom. So I want to be a judge like you and sit while I work.

I am watching all of the television programs that show how a judge does the job. I am ready any time you need me.

Please call me when you need to hire a sistant judge. I can come in after school each day. I have Girl Scouts on Saturday and church on Sunday.

Andrea A.

Dear Judge,

96. Dear Judge,

My mom and I have been waiting for this to be finished for two years. We didn't do anything. We didn't go any place. We didn't even unpack our boxes. We only waited so we could go home.

You were supposed to make every thing right. I don't know what happened.

You were supposed to let us move back and start a new life. But you decided to leave things as they are. Well they aren't.

We don't like it here. We don't know anyone here. We just wait around for my father to pick me up or not pick me up. I just feel sad when he takes me.

We have a real life waiting for us in Troy with grandma and grandpa Wells. We have all my cousins and most of our stuff. Mom has a really good job there and her college sweet heart wants us to marry him.

I feel like we are stuck in the middle of a huge empty field. Can you please change your mind. No one will think you are stupid if you change your mind. They will think you are smarter for listening.

Thank you,

Marsha R.

Children's Letters to the Judge

97. Dear Judge,

I promise You and God to never do this to my children.

Leigh

98. Dear Judge,

I have been a good student, son, brother and friend to the people around me. I hope you will consider letting me decide where I will live from now on. My parents are unable to come to an agreement and I feel they won't be able to move on until this situation is settled.

My father is a good man and father but feels I should go to the military boarding school that he and his father attended. The academy is close to his home and I think he would make sure I was able to spend scheduled time with both he and my mother according to the visitation order.

My mother is a good woman and mother and would like me to live with her and my two younger siblings. Mother has shown a willingness to make sure we are available for scheduled and special event visitation with our father.

The schooling with my mother would be less directed but just as excellent. I am inclined to stay with my siblings and mother for the support and family contact.

I have spoken to my parents and would appreciate instruction on what action I should take now to make my wishes known to the court.

Sincerely,

Chandler W.

Children's Letters to the Judge

99. Dear Judge,

I don't want to talk about this no more. Ever time someone talks things just get worsser. Yall don't no what you are doin.

Javy D.

Dear Judge,

100. Dear Judge,

This divorce stuff is getting easier. Everyone is calmed down and I get more stuff for birthday and Christmas than I did before.

At first I got away with more stuff cause my parents wouldn't talk to each other. That ended last summer after I got them each to pay for two weeks at summer camp. Four weeks at camp were cool but having to talk to them both in mom's kitchen after was not cool.

The biggest problem I have now is that what ever stuff I need is always at the house I am not at. You have probably fixed this stuff before so could you give my dad a call.

Sincerely,

Ben B.

Children's Letters to the Judge

101. Dear Judge,

I love my dad but could you have my mom come over and cook our food. Dad stinks at cooking. I think mom has time right after work and just before she goes to night school. I could do her homework while she cooks our dinner if that will help.

I think my mom and dad like each other better now than they did when she lived here with us. I think its cool but it is weird.

Baxter A.

102. Dear Judge,

Can I move in with the Browns. They have a nice family and so many kids they wont even notice one more kid.

My brother is going to live with dad. My sister is going to live with my mother. They get to decide where they want to live because they are in high school.

I would like to live with the Browns because they still have a family with a mother and a father. I am there most of the time if I am not at school.

I dont think my mom and dad would care.

Tom C.

Children's Letters to the Judge

103. Dear Judge,

My Dad said I used to be such a good boy and my brother was always a problem. I didn't even know they thought I was ever good.

Since Dad moved out they say I have turned into a monster. I guess they are right. I don't know why I do this stuff.

How bad does a kid have to be before you put them in jail. Do they make jail clothes in kid size? Can I get probition instead?

Yours forever,

Hudson A.

104. Dear Judge,

How do I get a divorce from my dad?

He doesn't want to be with my mom anymore but he can't stand it if mom starts to date other guys. They have been divorced for two years.

When Dad picks me up for visits he always makes my mom cry. He only calls me to find out what is going on with her. If I don't answer his questions he gets really mad.

He doesn't care about how I am doing or anything about spending time with me. I told him I did not want to talk to him on the phone or go with him. So he had the lawyer send mom a letter that said if she didn't let dad have contact with me she would go to jail.

It is getting worse all the time. If I could get a divorce from him, he might leave us alone. I don't have the money to get a lawyer. Any ideas?

Yours Truly,

Scott S.

Children's Letters to the Judge

105. Dear Judge,

My aunt Jane said you were probably grumpy in court today because you didnt have time to eat lunch. You should save some bacon and toast from your breakfast and put it together with peanut butter for lunch. It will taste real good and you will not feel grumpy.

Sincerely,

Abby F.

106. Dear Judge,

I asked my dad for a new bike. He said he pays a lot of money for child support. Dad said that the child support money he sends mom is mine and that I can spend it on anything I want.

Mom said that dad makes a lot of money and the support the court ordered is the bottom. She said the child support money is hers to get the things she thinks I need. If there is money left over I can have some of the things that I want. Mom said dad could afford to buy me the extra things I want.

Dad said mom spends the money on things she would have to buy even if I didnt live with her like house and car payment and the child support money should not be used to make her life easier.

Mom says the child support doesnt even cover my sentials and says the subject is closed. I think I have enuf sentials.

Can you tell me who is right? Is the child support money mine? Is it all my dad should have to pay? Is my mom using it right?

Thanks,

Jim B.

Children's Letters to the Judge

107. Dear Judge,

My mom says I look just like my dad.
She says I think just like my dad.
She says I will be tall just like my dad.
She says she loves me.
How can she love me when she says she hates him so much.

Sincerely,

Dane O.

108. Dear Judge,

I think you need to know something.

My parents called off the divorce again but they are hitting each other again.

They tell me to mind my own business cause I don't know what is really going on and I don't understand adult things. I know they are not supposed to hit each other.

My teacher said to take Jen and go to the neighbor when they start fighting. Last night we went out my window. Mrs. Parks said we could come anytime.

My dad came to get us this morning and told Mrs. Parks we were sleep walking. She told him it was never a problem and we could sleep walk to her house when ever we wanted to. He said that would be fine.

Your friend,

John T.

Children's Letters to the Judge

109. Dear Judge,

If my real mom lets me have candy in my backpack when I go for visitation can my step mom take it out with out my permission or a search warrant?

Sincerely,

Christian L.

110. Dear Judge,

I would like to know if my mommie ever loved me. She left us when I was little and I don't know what I did wrong.

I would like to talk to her about it. I think if I said was sorry and I wouldn't do anything wrong again maybe she would come back.

My dad is getting married again and then it will be too late. Linda is a nice lady and she wants to be our mommie. But I think I would like to have a chance to talk to my first mommie first.

If you can find my mommie call me tonight. I am going with Linda and sister to buy wedding dresses tomorrow.

Sincerely,

Elaine

Children's Letters to the Judge

111. Dear Judge,

My mom and I move all the time. I only liked one of the four schools I went to last year.

I do not see my dad or grandma or granddad Lasiter in three Christmases. I never have time to make friends and we don't have anyone we can call if we are sick or our car breaks down again.

We find a good place to start over but then have to leave when people start asking us questions.

I don't know where we did live but you could find it in our file. Please tell them we are ok and it would be better if they would stop looking for us and just let us alone. My mom really needs me and I want to stay with her. Please change the court papers.

Sincerely,

Tommy H.

Dear Judge,

112. Dear Judge,

I am in real trouble. The teacher moved Andrew to the other side of the room. Now I cant copy his papers and I will get bad grades again.

I will be grounded all the time and my dad will say I got my mom's brains again. I dont want him to think I am lazy and stupid and will grow up just like her.

If you know where my mom is can I go live with her. She is not really the way he says. Dad said he has custody because she wont give me all the vantages. It is ok with me. She thinks I am smart and pretty and she likes me better.

Sincerely,

Nicki

Children's Letters to the Judge

113. Dear Judge,

My grandpa says when he was little all the kids only had one mom and one dad and there wasnt no tv. He said it was better then.

Where did you go to see comercials when there wasnt no tv?

Grandpa said that just because my parents are big that doesnt mean they are grown up.

He promised as soon as they are grown up they will take care of me again. Grandma said he is telling me the truth.

Your friend,

Tony D.

Dear Judge,

114. Dear Judge,

I will be eighteen next week and want to thank you for the time and interest you have given me.

I know the luckiest day of my life was when you were assigned to decide who would have custody of me. As you learned later, I was actually outside sleeping in the backseat of my father's car in the summer heat for the 4 hours my parents were in court.

You were able to see that neither of my parents would or could care for me without intense supervision. Therefore, for the last eight years of my life I was brought to the courthouse and visited you four times each year in your chambers. You checked the folder I brought with my current medical, school records and notes from my teachers. You talked to me and listened while you review the status of my custody. You were the only adult who really cared about me.

I know that what you did for me was not required of you and that you didn't get any extra pay for it.

I have seen lots of other kids fall through the cracks. Thank you for saving my life and guiding my parents as they raised me. Without your warnings, threats and guidance my parents would have made a monster out of me.

I have finished high school and have applied to a culinary institute to train as a chef.

I intend to stay on the path you have kept me on and will show my appreciation for your efforts by being the kind of person you have shown me I can be.

Thank you,

Marty

Children's Letters to the Judge

115. Dear Judge,

I wish there was no such of a thing as divorce.

Karl

Dear Judge,

116. Dear Judge,

Dear Mom,
Dear Dad,
Dear Attorneys,

Thought you might want to see your grades before they went home to your parents. Since there has been little effort on your part to improve, we feel you will have to repeat many of the basic classes.

	Report Card
Paying Attention	S-
Attitude	F
Getting Along With Others	S-
Finishing Your Assignments On Time	S-
Behaving Responsibly	S-
Learning From Your Mistakes	F
Attendance	S
Homework	S-
Taking Responsibility For Your Actions	F
Adapting To New Situations	F
Displaying Proper Anger Management	F
Keeping Promises	F
Effort To Improve	S-

Marshal M.

Children's Letters to the Judge

117. Dear Judge,

The girls at school asked me to go skating with them but we don't have the money because we don't get my child support.

Could you do something to help us? We need the money.

Not just for skating but for shoes and school clothes and really important things.

We only got a check three times. I won't be old enough to baby sit till next summer.

Thank you for your help,

Erica

Dear Judge,

118. Dear Judge,

Get a clue. My dad does not take care of me here. My stepmom is supposed to and she isn't any happier about it than I am. She is only twelve years older than me and doesn't have any opinion my dad hasn't given her.

She hates having to be seen with me. She makes sure everyone she talks to knows she isn't old enough to have a teenager. She won't say anything to dad because she likes the credit cards and lifestyle.

My dad works all the time and just wanted custody so he wouldn't have to pay money to my mom.

He says if I leave my stuff stays with him and he won't pay for college. I don't care any more.

I need to see my mother more than every other weekend. How old do I have to be to get the court to listen to me?

Sincerely,

Elizabeth R.

Children's Letters to the Judge

119. Dear Judge,

I dont care what anyone says. I am going to be just like my dad when I grow up.

Patrick

Dear Judge,

120. Dear Judge,

My little brother thinks it will help if we send you a letter. I don't think it will but I guess it is worth a try.

Our parents are totally out of control. Dad is living with some bimbo from his office and mom is dating a real jerk. They say the meanest things about each other and use words we get grounded for.

I spend more time taking care of my brother than either of them and I'm not ready for the job. I just want to be a normal kid again.

Our parents say things are better now than when they were together but that is totally a lie. My brother and I dont have any idea of where we are going to be from one day to the next or what will happen next week.

We think we would be better off at Grams in California. We both have savings bonds that aunt Debbie has given us for the last three years to pay for the tickets.

Call or e-mail me at my school account.

Thanks tons,

Cass and Mike

Children's Letters to the Judge

121. Dear Judge,

Dont you care how I feel?

Joshua E.

122. Dear Judge,

Can you ask God to help my mom.

My dad says that since she is not a christian she is going to burn in hell for ternity. I love my mom and have asked Jesus to save her but my dad said that wont help. He said she has to accept Jesus in her heart to be saved.

Mom said she will be just fine cause God loves her to.

Since your are old and very important could you please talk to God for me. I worry about my mom all the time.

Thank you very very much,

Janice J.

Children's Letters to the Judge

123. Dear Judge,

Since our parents started having trouble they don't have any time for me.

My big brother Dan lets me hang out with him.

They make cigarettes out of marijuana and steal from the grogery store.

I am scared.

Jarred L.

Dear Judge,

124. Dear Judge,

We started a kids court. We have a desk for the judge, a chair for the witnes, two tables and four chairs for the sides and eight chairs for the jury. We don't have twelve because we don't have enough kids on the block.

When a kid has a problem or has done something bad we open kids court. We put the ten parts that other people get to be on paper. The kid that has to go to court and the person on the other side already have their parts. The rest of us take a paper out of the vase and that tells you what part you have to do.

We only do kids court on Saturday cause we all school and stuff. The first week we had five cases. Now sometimes we don't have any and usually we have two.

A mom wants to bring a kid from the next block to our court. Can we do that?

Thanks,

Whitney B.
I been the judge four times.

Children's Letters to the Judge

125. Dear Judge,

When I grow up I am going to be a wrestler so no one can hurt my momie no more.

Mick

Dear Judge,

126. Dear Judge,

So my parents sent me to that shrink you told them to and now they both say he stinks. He doesn't stink. He gave me the words to say to be ok.

This is the list of what I am allowed to say.

- It is not fair for you to attempt to put me in that position.
- I am not comfortable with what you are asking me to do.
- I am not comfortable with what you are telling me.
- I don't want to make a decision about this subject.
- I am not an adult and this is an adult subject.
- I am sorry you feel that way.
- Please don't say those things about someone I love. I don't let anyone talk that way about you.

I like Mr. Bondholder and would like to keep talking to him.

Thank you,

Frank B.

Children's Letters to the Judge

127. Dear Judge,

You should only smile.

When I saw you I was afraid of you because you were wareing a big black dress and your face has a bunch of ruffles and you look like a mean monster.

When you smile all the ruffles look very friendly.

Leland

Dear Judge,

128. Dear Judge,

I have never liked school until now. I went to the counselor about the trouble I was having at home.

Miss. Chow said my problems were real and important but that I had to pull myself out of only concentrating on myself. She got me assigned to the school newspaper and my job is to review books that deal with issues that concern students. I have a special interest in children and their feelings when their parents are getting a divorce. This extra curricular activity has raised my grade in literature from a C- to an A. Cool hu?

I would like to do a Divorce Newsletter for other kids in divorce. I have included an example of what I have in mind. It includes articles by other staff members and reviews of a couple of movies and these books: What Can I Do?, It's Not Your Fault, Koko Bear, Kids Advice to Kids and Helping Children Survive Divorce.

Please contact our student advisor Mr. Franklin at Central High School if you have any questions. He said he would assist us with this project.

Thank you,

Linda S.

Children's Letters to the Judge

129. Dear Judge,

If you had to start as the person who sweeps the floor and work your way up to judge by doing a good job at everything they gave you, and had to keep doing a good job to stay a judge, you would still be sweeping the floors.

Gary R.

Dear Judge,

130. Dear Judge,

Mom and dad are very different in lots of ways. Dad is still very angry with mom since she left him. Dad wants us kids to hate mom. He thinks we won't love him if we love mom. When we do something wrong or that reminds him of mom he yells, you are just like your mother, this means we are really horrible.

I look like mom and I am the oldest girl and I am very close with mom and I help with the little kids at home and at dads. I know what to do to take care of them and he doesn't like me to decide. Dad is at work most of the day and does not know what to feed them or when to put them in bed.

Mom said he has a lot of issues and that I may be reminding him of the pain of us all leaving. My brothers and sisters still are upset about the last time dad and I were yelling at each other. Mom said I can't yell at dad or any other adult. Mom said I should try to reminding him of the ways that I am like him so he is not feeling so threatened. I think it will be easier when school starts again. Dad always liked helping me with math and science projects. Mom said that seeking his advice and participation would help show him that he hasn't lost us to her.

Mom said I am not responsible for what happened between them or for fixing it. She said I could help by being the best me I could be and tell him I am glad he is my dad and show him I respect him and tell him I love him.

I have been doing what mom said and what you said in your office. It is taking a long time but I think you are right. We still need mom and dad and they need us.

Sincerely,

Lindsey, James, Michael, Daniel, Seth B.

Children's Letters to the Judge

131. Dear Judge,

You could really help me by sending me a copy of my parent's divorce papers. Now that our holidays and weekends are divided between our parents it is hard for us to arrange our activities or make any plans.

With a list of when we are supposed to be where, I could make a calendar for us to check before we make plans. Actually I would make two one for each house.

Our parents are dealing with so many of their own worries that they can't seem to remember we need to know the new system. The calendars would actually take away some of the arguments.

If you don't have the papers, please let me know who to call.

Sincerely,

Hank G.

Dear Judge,

132. Dear Judge,

I hate moving back and forth each month. This may be ok for my parents, the lawyers and you, but is stinks for me. I have talked to my parents, counselor at school and to my teachers. No one is listening. I can't keep up my grades, and I am really miserable.

I don't even want to hear another of you say, Well there is nothing I can do about this.

Somebody better get this straightened out or I will and none of you are going to like it. And it will make you all look as stupid as you are.

Jacob D.

Children's Letters to the Judge

133. Dear Judge,

We had to write what we did this summer so I wrote about our divorce.

Miss Lichtenwalter gave me a 100 on my paper.

Miss Lichtenwalter said she was going to read it in front of the class. I wanted to hide my head.

When she finished reading my story the class was real quiet. Miss Lichtenwalter asked if anyone had any thoughts about what the story meant to them and if would share their feelings.

Lots of people said it made them sad. Some said the had the same trouble in there family and it helped them to know that I had the same thing. Almost everyone already knew other kids like me.

Miss Lichtenwalter said she read my story to the teachers in the teachers lounge and it made them cry.

I feel kind of funny but I feel better. You should tell kids to write about their divorce and feel better too.

Wyatt

Dear Judge,

134. Dear Judge,

Mom said I have to wait for your answer. Can I take my cat to Canada when I go for summer visit?

Megan

Children's Letters to the Judge

135. Dear Judge,

My dad says there is a right and wrong way to do everything. He doesn't care if you can get the same results a different way. The home evaluation woman says that my dad's not able to be flexible and that is not good for me.

I like living with my dad because I can depend on him and our house. We eat dinner at the same time each night and go to church every Sunday. I can have friends spend the night on Friday and I am always home on Tuesday nights in case my mom calls.

Dad always remembers to come to my school events and lets me do all the sports except football. He never forgets to make sure there is money in my lunch account at school. My dad says my homework is my responsibility and he reads the newspaper at the table while I do my homework.

People like my mom better than my dad because she is everyones best friend. Sometimes we eat dinner right after school and other times not until bedtime. When she forgets to do the wash we stop at Walmart to get me something clean to put on for school. If she sleeps late I don't make it to school that day. Mom doesn't like schedules because they inhibit the flow of life. Everyone says my mom is interesting and exciting.

I need to live where I have been living. When things are exciting all the time I get nervous.

Thank you,

Brad E.

Dear Judge,

136. Dear Judge,

I started a kids lawyers club. We could come to court for the kids. You already have grown-up lawyers for grownups. But they dont get paid by the kids so they dont listen to the kids. We dont get paid by the kids either because they usually dont have no money.

I think having kids lawyers for the kids is a good idea. I am very good at telling when people are telling the truth so I am a good kids lawyer.

Please send me any information I will need to do this.

Respectfully yours,

Mark H.

PS
When I grow up I will be happy to help out with some of the grownups but I will still listen to the kids.

Children's Letters to the Judge

137. Dear Judge,

This system stinks. It's like all of us are walking around waiting for you to decide which part of us isn't worth keeping. It would still hurt allot, but could you find a faster way?

We weren't ever a happy family but we were a whole family. We won't ever be a whole anything ever again. I don't even know if each of us can be whole people again.

Big things, little things, nothing is good any more. I don't know if it ever will be. Like you really care.

Sincerely,

Ricki V.

138. Dear Judge,

I fly to my mom's for spring break, summer Thanksgiving and Christmas. Mom pays for my ticket to her house and my dad pays for my ticket home.

I am always on the same airline. I think I should get the frequent flyer miles since I do all the traveling. I think I should get to decide what I want to do with the points. I have enough for two round trips any place in the world cause I been traveling for eleven years now.

The flyer reports come to me at my dad's house cause that's where I really live. I already called the airline to make sure they don't expire and they said I was the one who owned the points.

Is there a court order about this that would help me?

Your friend,

Jeff G.

Children's Letters to the Judge

139. Dear Judge,

First I want you to decide cause my parents cant. Then I do not want you to take so long cause theere is so much trouble and I think if you decide everything will be back. The guy that lives next door is real old. He sais that things take as long as they take and some times you need to just sit back and watch cause it is not your job. Now I see that it needs to take a long time so my parents will get done being mad at each othere. We are the first ones in the family to get divorced so we aint to good at it. The old man said he did not get old by being dum so I will do what he sais.

Demitus

Dear Judge,

140. Dear Judge,

Would you just tell my dad to leave me alone.

He calls and makes a big deal about picking me up for the weekend and then does not show up or call.

This is not a one time deal it happens all the time.

I am really tired of this shit. I do not want to talk to him or see him any more. I don't care where he is or what happens to him.

I do not give a dam what you or my mother say. I am not talking to him or going to see him again.

When I was little I would cry cause he did not come. Not any more.

I got a list of all the times he stood me up and I am putting it on my front door, taking it to the neighbors, my teacher, counselor and the dean of boys.

If he tries to make me go with him I will call the police.

James S.

Children's Letters to the Judge

141. Dear Judge,

It doesn't hurt any more. It doesn't feel any more.

Adelle

Dear Judge,

142. Dear Judge,

    I love school and my favorite teacher is Miss. Lemley. I stay after school to wipe the black board and put the chairs on the desks. If she has papers to grade she lets me sit at my desk to do my homework. I go to school early so I can sit with her at the teachers table and eat breakfast. I walk home real slow and I go the long way.

    My Mom lets me ride to the early service at church with the Jacobsons and then I stay for Sunday school and children's church and the regular service. The people are real nice to me and they are nice to each other. I help serve lunch to the old people and the Wood's family drop me off at home at 1:30 in the afternoon.

    On Friday I ride the with bus home with Becky and we have dinner. Her parents take us to the Girl Scout meeting and ice cream. Lots of times I get to spend the weekend.

    Grandma and Gramps Clifton let me spend the night and sometimes I go to Aunt Gina.

It isn't nice being at home.

Sincerely,

Samantha

Children's Letters to the Judge

143. Dear Judge,

We are not allowed to talk about our mom. We would like to live with her because she is probably very rich and really misses us and loves us. Don't tell dad what we decided.

Dear Judge,

144. Dear Judge,

Would you tell us what is going on. None of the grown ups will talk to us. Mom and dad say we didn't do anything and they love us all. We talked about it and we think we musta done something. They always were fighting because of us and we are trying to be very good.

Andre started wetting the bed again and we are trying to help him stop and clean it up each morning. Becky is bitting her nails till they bleed and my stomach hurts all the time. Katie and Jen are just scared.

Since I am the biggest they think I can get us some help. I think we are much better children now and would like you to help us. If you will fix this we won't ask for anything for Christmas.

Yours very truly,

Mark and Katie and Jennie and Becky and Andre

Children's Letters to the Judge

145. Dear Judge,

Tell my dad's girlfriend to stop walking around the house naked when my dad isn't home.

I have tried to tell my dad, but he thinks Heather is an angel and that if I am seeing things it is because I am spying on her.

Heather tried to get my dad to take the lock off my door so I wouldn't die if the house burned down. I got a smoke detector for my room and dad said it would be fine.

I told my friend Mac when it started and he thought it was cool now he even thinks its gross.

I can't say anything to mom because she has just calmed down and will go nuts again.

Try to take care of it today if you can.

Sincerely,

Brad

Dear Judge,

146. Dear Judge,

For 12 years I have been going to visitation just like you ordered. Last summer I spent 6 weeks at my mom's. I called her a couple of months before summer to ask her if she would get my ticket for two weeks later than usual and I would stay two weeks later than usual. I have worked very hard at karate to qualify for the Nationals in Florida. She said, No, I already bought the ticket." She wouldn't let dad pay for the change in the tickets. I was so disappointed that I cried and I don't cry much. I got my ticket and she bought it only one month before I came. Mom's trailer is in the desert and the subdivision does not have a club house, game room, swimming pool, or activities. I only saw other kids once. Mom's boyfriend and his 18 year old son live with mom and her four year old son. Mom works all the time but the boyfriend and his son don't. I was either baby sitting the little boy or alone in the living room because the boyfriend would keep the little boy locked in the bedroom with him while he slept off his sick headaches all day. I called my dad and stepmom about 14 times each just to talk. After 11 days I asked my stepmom to send me my skateboard. She called from Wal-Mart to fill the room in the box. She put 4 kinds of cereal, fruit roll-ups, pop tarts, cashew nuts, snacks, and chips I asked for and some things she suggested. She spent 70 bucks. My stepmom called me back to say she sent it in c/o of mom at the Post Office so I would have it in 2-3 days. I told mom that the whole time I was there the 18 year old would punch me when I walked past. It hurt and left me black and blue. Mom said he was just playing. My dad called to see if I got my package but mom took my cell phone away and didn't let me call home again. Mom said my package never came. When I got back home the post office sent us proof that my mom signed for my box. She never gave it to me. I am tired of getting lied to, beat up and stolen from. I am not going back.

Joshua

Children's Letters to the Judge

147. Dear Judge,

I can not tell you my name because I do not want you to know who I am until after you answer my question.

My parents got a divorce. After a bunch of stupid stuff my dad got custody of us.

After three months my dad dropped us off at moms for Saturday and Sunday and never came back to get us. After that Dad's cell phone number does not work any more and they say he does not work at the store any more.

It is good here and we want to stay here with mom. Mom still pays money out of her paycheck for us. Mom says we should stay quite and not say something.

Can dad come to take us back after we have been here with mom for the rest of the summer and all the school time?

Leave the answer with Miss Purdy at Jackson Elementary School she knows who I am but wont tell.

Dear Judge,

148. Dear Judge,

It is better now. It is not what I wanted. But, it is better now. Mom has lost 65 pounds and my grades are back up to B's.

Dad is still working for the hospital and they may put him on staff permanently.

We can see that my big sister hasn't cut herself in weeks and doesn't mind us asking.

You said you wanted to keep in touch so that's all for now.

Sincerely,

Elizabeth B.

Children's Letters to the Judge

149. Dear Judge,

Well everyone has everything they want but me. Mom gets to go be an important executive. Dad gets custody of me. I get zip.

I am thirteen and think you should take my needs in to account. At school I am not a preppie or a kicker. I am a skater. We don't do drugs like people think we do. We just choose big clothes because they are comfortable and cool looking.

Dad tells me stupid stuff like, if I walk like a duck and talk like a duck and hang around with ducks, I am a duck. My dad treats me like a baby. I have to leave my bedroom door unlocked unless I am changing clothes. He made me take stuff about casting spells against your enemies off my web site and won't let me get my tongue pierced like my best friend has. Dad makes me explain the lyrics to the songs I listen to. He says he can't make out or understand my music. He takes some of my CD's away. He checks up on me all the time.

Mom said that dad has her backing for any decisions about me.

Dad took me to talk to our pastor to talk about my future. Pastor said my dad is just doing what's best for me. Pastor is clueless. I don't want be like my parents or do the jobs they do, And I don't need good grades. I am not going to college. I don't need to college to be a Paranormal Event Investigator.

I hope you can do something to help me out. This is really a drag.

Later,

Dark Raven (Julia R.)

Dear Judge,

150. Dear Judge,

You sent my parents to a class called, Parenting Through A Divorce. I think it helped them.

It would really help if you had a class called, How To Go Through Your Parents Divorce.

If you need some advice about what to put in the class I would be happy to help you. I think it would help children.

Yours very truly,

Belinda D.

Children's Letters to the Judge

151. Dear Judge,

We know you don't remember my twin brother and me but we remember you. My mother wanted me to live with her and my dad wanted Andy to live with him. We are really glad you didn't let them separate us.

We have been keeping a diary. I write in blue and Samantha writes in red just like this letter. When we started our new diary for this year we decided to look at the first one we did.

We forgot that the first June we were making a plan to run away from home and live in a train car like the Box Car Kids. Lots of stuff that was real serious to us then is funny now.

We know that our diaries and having each other to talk to has helped us through the hard parts. We hope you have kept all the kids that want to stay together in a family together. They really need each other.

We thank you again,

Samantha and Andrew C.

Dear Judge,

152. Dear Judge,

My mom won't let me call my grandmother any more. Since my grandfather died last year my mother has gotten meaner and meaner to her mother. Mom says she hates her mother and is even saying grandmother and grandfather beat her and did weird stuff to her and her sisters when they were small.

My aunts say it didn't happen. Now even they aren't allow to call or come here any more.

I don't know what to do about my mom. She stopped all contact with dad and dad's family when they got a divorce and now she doesn't want any contact with our family.

If we call any of our grandparents we get screamed at and grounded. It is really lonely after spending so much time with our cousins and family.

One of my aunts is trying to get the family together to do something about mom. It will just make things worse. I don't know what you can do but we need help.

Arnie

Children's Letters to the Judge

153. Dear Judge,

i am sory my brothr is sory so is my sister we wont be bad no mor send my daddy hom and we wil be hapi

chris
cammie
carl

Dear Judge,

154. Dear Judge,

My mother told us awful things about our dad all our lives. She made us hate him as much as she did for a long time.

We said lots of mean things to him and about him to other people. We would say anything mom told us to say.

I just wanted to tell you that the things we told you that our dad did, were a lie. We don't know why we said those things but we did. We are sorry and want you to know it.

Both of my sisters are in college now and I will be finishing high school this year. When finals are done I am calling my dad to pick me up. I am tired of living with my mom's anger, hate and lies. I don't care if I ever see my mother after that. I tried to leave when my sisters left but they talked me into staying until I finished high school. My sisters don't even talk to mom when they call me.

I want to live with him and my step-mother. He is and always was a good man. My step-mother is a real nice person and cares about all of us. I just wanted you to know.

Sincerely,

Jason E.

Children's Letters to the Judge

155. Dear Judge,

Thank you for letting me get to know my dad. I don't remember having a dad before now. I get to do more stuff than before and my mom shows up for everything now.

Ron

Dear Judge,

156. Dear Judge,

I would like the phone number of a judge in Hollywood. My best friend Emily says that's where they make the television shows. She said the families on television are happy because they dont just make life up each day when they get out of bed. They have people that write a script that tells them what to say and do each day.

I would like a judge in Hollywood to make a happy family script for us. I think we would move to Hollywood if we have to live there to get that judge. It hasnt been nice here for a long time and I think we should try anything.

Please send a map from Lansing to Hollywood. My dad could probably drive us there this afternoon.

Love and kisses,

Marie I.

Children's Letters to the Judge

157. Dear Judge,

I would like to trade the next Christmasses Thanksgivins Easters Valentines Birthdays Forth of Julyes and Holoweens four 100 years

if you will just put things back the way it was.

I think we could all forget how things are now really fastly.

My grandpa says you have to be willn to give up something to get somethn else you really want. If I didn't give enough just let me no cause I still have some real nice stuff.

Thank You,

Cloie C.

Dear Judge,

158. Dear Judge,

You were right. Jason does not like military school but we are all doing much better with him gone. He is doing better to.

Mother says she will practice before you again but it will take some time. Father reminded mother that she always felt you were fair with her clients so why couldn't she see you were fair with her. Father says he knew it was the right decision when you made it. That is why you always see him in your court.

I miss Jason but if he had been sent away to school sooner I don think my parents would have to be divorced.

Respectfully,

Sheilah D.

Children's Letters to the Judge

159. Dear Judge,

Me an my brother are adopted. They had to be a mom and a dad to get us. Mom and dad are getting a divorce and we will probably be unadopted.

I didn't live any place cept the hospital before I was adopted. Lotar was with a bunch of families before we got him and he thinks one of them will take him back. I don't think the hospital will take me back. I don't have a job to get a house.

They didn't say something so maybe you could divorce them and let them keep us.

Stanley

Dear Judge,

160. Dear Judge,

I have a close relationship with both of my parents and do not want to hurt either of their feelings.

I believe both parents have done the best they could to provide for me and my siblings.

However, I do wish to live with my mother on a full-time basis. Mom and her husband have a farm in the state of South Dakota.

These are my reasons:

A. I don't particularly like the school that I attend in Arizona and the living situation with my father's uncle, whom I believe has a drinking problem.

B. I would enjoy living with my mother and her husband on their farm near Goodwin, South Dakota.

C. I would like to attend school in South Dakota.

D. I want to live nearer to my relatives, grandparents, uncles and aunts and cousins that live in the state of South Dakota.

E. I want to continue to have a close relationship with my father and I know my mother would allow frequent contacts with him and his family as often as I desire.

F. I love equally both of my parents however I believe and so do my siblings believe that we would be better off and happier if we live in South Dakota with my mother and her husband.

Thank you for considering this request. I have sent a copy to both of my parents attorney's.

Blondie J.

Children's Letters to the Judge

161. Dear Judge,

I will be 16 in 3 months and want to live with Dwayne my boyfriend. We have been seeing each other for 4 months and are in love. He is 22 and a great guy and has a good job at the grocery store and an apartment.

I am pregnant so you can see that I am not a child any more. I don't need to finish high school because I am going to be a house wife and take care of our children.

When I explained this to my mom she was totally ballistic and unreasonable. I told her I was only telling her to be polite. It is time for me to start my own family and I will do a much better job than she did.

We were screaming at each other and the nosey woman next door called the police. I was really mad and told them some stuff to get mom in trouble. They didn't do anything except to tell us that Child Protecting Services was going to check on what I said.

I want to be emancipated instead of living with my mom or dad. If you can't make my mom understand I will just have to leave. If I can't be with Dwayne my life will be ruined.

Sincerely,

Madison M.

Dear Judge,

162. Dear Judge,

Kacie said you are the same judge that she had for her divorce and I should not worry. Kacie and her momie made me a divorce backpack with a doll, a flashlight, a address book, a new toothbrush with a little baby tooth paste, some bandaids, a new hair brush, a coloring book, markers, a picture frame with room for mom and dad. Kacie said I will be ok.

Love,

Clarice

Children's Letters to the Judge

163. Dear Judge,

Thank you for letting me live with my grandmother. The foster care family was very nice but they were not my family.

I don't think I will ever understand why my dad killed my mom. Mrs. Morrison at the lawyers office said she will always be available at no cost to help my grandmother and me plan my future. I think she feels responsible. I know grandmother and I wish we could have done something to change things.

I just wanted you to know we are alright.

Yours truly,

Emma

Dear Judge,

164. Dear Judge,

    My dad and my granny don't like each other any more. Cause my granny is on moms side and dad said most everything is grannys fault and granny said dad was never no good. Dad says granny would not throw old dish water on us if we was on fire next to her house.

    I remember when they all laughed together and huged each other every time we all came to grannys house.

    I didn't like it when they talk bad so I put my ear mufs on. When they start talking bad and when I don't have my ear mufs I go stand in the bathroom.

    Ever body talked to me about my ear mufs and I said I will put on my ear mufs from now on. I dont have to stand in the bathroom or put on my ear mufs very much now.

    Landon M.

Children's Letters to the Judge

165. Dear Judge,

I am writing to you because my parents stopped listening to me when they split up.

Even since I can remember when our parents took us to visit people we didn't like they would say, "You don't have to love these people. But you do have to be polite to them. It's just good manners."

Now that they are divorced they don't even have good manners with each other. I feel just like they did when I was a kid. They don't have to love each other, but they should at least be polite to each other. Even if they have to pretend for us. It would make us feel lots better.

There are about twenty of us in my homeroom class at junior high school that are having the same problem. I just told you that so you would know that if you can do something about this it would be helping a bunch of us.

Thank you,

Brian M.

166. Dear Judge,

Ya'll think you are so smart. I know how to make it stop hurting. Dad drinks beer till he passes out. Then we can do what ever we want and you know what he don't even notice when the hard stuff goes away. He thinks his friends drink too much. We don't hurt either. The joke is he looks awful in the morning and we look fine.

Hugh

Children's Letters to the Judge

167. Dear Judge,

I would like to live with my Dad. It is much better there. I don't have to go to bed till I make the decision that I am ready for rest. I am trusted to do homework. My room is my room and I don't have to keep it at grownup standards. The cleaning service takes care of the chores. And Dad takes me to lots of very very nice places I would not normally get to go to.

When I told my Dad I wanted to live with him he gave me a big hug and said he loved me. It made me feel really good. I know it will make him happy if you let me move.

When I told my Mom I wanted to live with my Dad she cried and then got disscusted with me. I told her it would made Dad very happy and make me happy. My Mom said that my Dad never did live in the real world.

When Mom got done ben disscusted with me she said I could write you a letter. And she would do what ever you said.

I told Dad about Mom was going to let me send you a letter. He gave me a big hug and kiss and said not to hold my breath. My Dad said everything was fine and that he would love me no matter where you let me live.

I would still have my stuff at my Moms house cause I will still love her two.

Your friend,

Isador

Dear Judge,

168. Dear Judge,

I feel like nobody can see me anymore.

Lacy H.

Children's Letters to the Judge

169.　Dear Judge,

I would like you to trash my first letter.

I ran away and the police arrested me and my boyfriend Jens. He will probably lose his job and he might go to jail.

When the police asked me questions I told them that mom beat me up and did dope with me. After they talked to my mom they took me to a place they called a Youth Crisis Center. It's really a kid jail. I thought they were going to arrest my mom for child abuse or something. They did ask her questions for almost three hours.

I was scared pretty good being in that place cause there were some really bad kids. One girl even put another girls head through the wall. I saw more of that place than I ever want to. Guess I was headed down the wrong road. I don't want to be in that place again. The officer that checked me out said that if I run away or get into trouble again, I will go to juvenile hall next time. She said juvie is much worse that the Crisis Center. Then the next step is real jail with adults.

My mom is going to keep me out of school for the rest of the week so we can work on fixing our relationship. We are going to counseling twice a week. Last night was a good night.

Cynthina J.

Dear Judge,

170. Dear Judge,

Can I just live at my school? We rote a story about our summer and Miss Baker moved my desk up to the front row. They really like me there and it is safe. I always go early and stay as late as they let me. I even get a nice breakfast.

Maryellen

Children's Letters to the Judge

171. Dear Judge,

I am in big trouble cause of my A that Miss Shell gave me. When I was writing about what I did this summer it was easy to write my paper and when I got a A for my paper I was happy and when my dad and my stepmom saw my paper and my A I was happy but when my mom saw my A and my paper I got in trouble.

My mom said that I should have said that I liked my summer at her house and that I had a good time and that I want to live there all the time and I love my stepdad and my stepsister and she took me to lots of fun places and spends lots of time with me and it is better than my dads house.

But when I told Miss Shell that my mom was mad at me because of what I said on my paper and that I had to fix it Miss Shell said my paper was just right and that I should always write about the way I see things not the way other people tell me to see things and I should be proud of my A and to tell my mom that once a paper is graded it can not be changed. I do not want to talk to mom about it could you?

T.C.

Dear Judge,

172. Dear Judge,

Why did you send me to live with my dad? What did I do wrong?

Riki

Children's Letters to the Judge

173. Dear Judge,

It is great visiting my dad. He is a slob and I get to be a slob when I am there and I get to sleep in my clothes.

Bo

Dear Judge,

174. Dear Judge,

    Please let me stay with my mother. We don't live in the car anymore. We live in a real nice place with a kitchen and everything. The apartment house is the same place my mother works. Mrs. Marston said mom is doing a great job and that they are going to keep her. Mr. Readheart mother's probation officer said he would be able to talk with you anytime you need him. He thinks mother is on the right track and I am an important stabilizing element in her life.

    I am much happier with mother than I am with my grandparents. They are sure my mother is never going to straighten out and they say awful things about her all the time. When they are displeased with me they say I am going to turn out just like my mother.

    My mother is a good person and really loves me. I go to her AA meetings with her and she goes with me to all of my team sports and my school events and church and helps me with my homework. My attendance and grades are still good. I asked Mrs. Jacob to talk to you if you call the school.

    There are only two of us but we are a real family and help each other. Next year I will be old enough to choose where I want to live. Please leave me here on the same temporary order from six months ago. My grandparents don't care that we are really doing very good together. My mother and I are sure you will help.

Sincerely,

Rhonda F.

Children's Letters to the Judge

175. Dear Judge,

It is hard to remember what my dad looks like and remember that he loves me.

Danny

Dear Judge,

176. Dear Judge,

Thank you for helping my mom and dad not have a divorce. Now I need you to fix this problem of my mom and dad divorcing my Mema an Papa.

Dad said they were the cause of all our troubles. Cause they were helping my mom when we lived with them because mom and dad were divorcing. Bailey and me did not know that.

Mema and Papa can not come here or call anymore. I think they will be good if you tell them they have to be good. They live on the block in the back of our block and I can not go there any more.

I miss them so much. Call them and call dad.

Brandon and Bailey

Children's Letters to the Judge

177. Dear Judge,

At Safe Haven Visitation Center I asked my real mom why she didn't send me a birthday gifts. She said she always sent me presents for Christmas and birthday. I told her I never got any. So she named a bunch of dolls, books and games she sent to me. I thought my dad got them for me. Mom said each one has a star drawn or sewn on everything she has ever sent me.

In my stuff there was a star drawn in almost all of my books and sewn into alot of my clothes and dolls. I did not say nothing to my dad or Patty.

I just want you to know.

Bye,

Carmella

Dear Judge,

178. Dear Judge,

I really need some help. My mom is a dancer and works at night so her boyfriend (whoever that happens to be this month) watches me at night. Some of her boyfriends have been real creeps, some have been ok and some just sleep and eat when she is not home.

Lots of stuff happened to me when I was small but I don't put up with anything anymore. I need you to help me find my father who left when my mom became a dancer. Mom said she had to become a dancer because her life was so dull and dad did not make enough money.

The stuff my mom tells me is dull I think would be nice. I need a dull life and I think my father would like to see me again now that my mom can't stop me from talking to him.

Thank you in advance,

Malane

Children's Letters to the Judge

179. Dear Judge,

I have lived with my mom since she and dad got divorced when I was 2. We never talked much about him either way. Last summer I told mom I wanted to meet dad. She wasn't very excited about it but she arranged for him to call me.

It was so cool talking to him on the phone. I told him I wanted to see him in person because I only saw him in wedding pictures and my baby pictures. He finally said OK. Dad picked me up for dinner at a fancy restaurant. He opened the car door for me at my house and the restaurant, held my chair.

When he took me home I told mom I wanted to spend every other weekend with dad. She looked uncomfortable but said, 'fine'. I met Annette, dad's girlfriend and Matt, his friend who had the other bedroom at the apartment. I slept on the couch in the living room. Matt would watch TV with me after dad and Annette would go to bed. Dad and Annette and me and Matt started to go everywhere together.

After a month of visits and a week of arguing with mom, I changed my visits to every weekend. I told her I really needed more time with dad. Everything was really cool and everyone treated me like an adult. Then one of mom's friends called. She saw me at a nightclub so made-up she had to look twice to make sure and that I was being inappropriate with a grown man

When I got home, I had to tell mom everything about dad's and she went ballistic saying that, "Matt, Dad and Annette could go to jail for what had been going on for almost a year". After she talked to dad he didn't try to call. As if he ever did. Mom said what was going on was wrong and that they had taken advantage of me instead of protecting me. I understand why mom feels the way she does and I feel really weird, ashamed and relieved at the same time. I don't know if I will ever want to see dad again.

Ruby

Dear Judge,

180. Dear Judge,

I am the oldest of four kids and feel that it is my responsibility to make sure we get through this. When our parents sat us down and explained that they were getting a divorce we all cried. Then it didn't seem real because they are still both here. In the beginning it was only until they could afford for one of them to move out and they weren't very clear about which one that would be. This divorce has been going on for a year and a half. Dad lives in the guest room on the second floor next to mine and mom lives in their old room. This usually works out pretty good but as things get closer to coming to an end Daisy and Andrew are having a really rough time.

They do a good job of being polite to each other and making sure we get to where we need to be. I don't think either one could handle it alone. Every so often it feels like if we don't say anything about it the divorce will go away. I know things don't go away if you ignore them.

I feel our parents have an obligation to care for us and that they should do what ever it takes to meet that obligation. I think we have the right to expect to be loved and live with both our parents. It should be the most important contract an adult has and they should have to complete it rather than be released from it by a divorce.

Having one of our parents move out of our home will be a great hardship for us and may cause serious long term damage to us emotionally. The children of this family are 'interested parties' in this matter and we ask to he heard.

Sincerely,

Richard, Donna, Andrew and Daisy

Children's Letters to the Judge

181. Dear Judge,

Funeral Notice

The remaining family members and friends of the Biglows gathered today to pay honor to and say good bye to a fine family. The Biglow family died Thursday June 15th of a divorce at the Clark County Courthouse after a painful illness of eight months. "It was a wonderful family and important part of the community." said Michael Havit, a long-time family friend. Many things caused the adult members of the family to reconsider their needs and values and helped propel the family into the broken-family spotlight. Our families are made of the parts of many other lives, so this loss will make many things happen in those lives. We hope some of those things will be happy.

Yes Judge, you missed the funeral. You really chopped us up and spit us out before you were done. But I guess the guy that kills something doesn't usually get to go to the graveside service.

We kids did dig a hole and burry a wooden box with things from our old life. Family photos from 9 Christmas, a picture of mom and dad dancing at John and Chris's wedding, the house key, paper dolls with each of our names on them and their hands taped together in a circle, certificate of appreciation from our church and 3 dog collars from dogs we had that have graves on the side yard.

We are just glad to be out from under your thumb.

We remain, What's left of the Biglows

Dear Judge,

182. Dear Judge,

I know you are going to be mad at me but I don't got no where else to go. When you took me from my family it really did help. I never was given a foster family but it was nice with Mrs. Whittiker and her staff. They tell me I have to leave here on my 17th birthday and I still ain't out of school yet and don't have a work permit. They invited me to still be part of group on Thursday night but I am pretty sure my father won't let me.

I am not afraid to go home and I know what is acceptable now and am able to say no. It is better for me to go home now since I have some little sisters that probably need me to protect them. As soon as I can I will make a real home for me and them.

Thank you for everything.

Shelly L.

Children's Letters to the Judge

183.   Dear Judge,

My sister is cutting herself again.

Swore I wouldn't tell anyone but its getting really bad. No one notices because she has always been quiet. It started when it got really shitty around here. Debbie cried when they started fighting then just stopped so I thought she was dealing. Then I saw her arm the same time dad did. Deb said her friends cat scratched her and dad bought it. I could tell they weren't scratches and told her to stop. She said she did it the first time just to see if she could feel anything anymore but now she can't stop because it makes her feel better.

I've tried everything. Deb says if I tell anyone she will disappear. She's almost gone now. We are all dying here in one way or another. Can't you do something to help.

Dustin S.

Dear Judge,

184. Dear Judge,

It is summer and I am at visitation and it's great.

You did a great job. I always knew I wanted to spend time with my dad and you made sure I could.

I am with my dad in his truck and we just spent a week in Alaska. We have a great big Red Kenworth with a huge sleeper and we pull a 53 foot dry van and I get to talk on the CB. We sit in the drivers area at the truck stop and I am marking the roads we drive on in my own atlas. We picked up our load in Arkansas and went through Missouri, Iowa, Minnesota. Then we had to pass through Customs at the Canada border and I saw real Mounties and through Manitoba, Saskatchewan, Alberta and British Columbia into the Yukon then into Alaska. We delivered our load in Anchoage and took a week of vacation time. We flew in an airplane and I got to sit up front with the pilot and fly the plane. Then we rode mountain bicycles and drove to the ocean to go deep sea fishing. We had the fish we caught sent my dads house and we are going to cook it when we get there.

On the way home we went south through British Columbia, back to Canada Customs then into Washington, Oregon and delivered in Sacramento, California. There we picked up a load to Denver, Colorado. Now we are waiting for another load and I just wanted to tell you how I was doing and thank you for everything.

Your Trucker Friend,

Sam

Children's Letters to the Judge

185. Dear Judge,

If I tell something bad will happen to us. Lots of people should know. But they don't even ask. When I am big I will help the children cause I know.

186. Dear Judge,

I got what I asked for. Turns out being on my own isn't as cool as I thought it would be. Divorced my parents both have to work more hours to pay their bills.

Even with the extra money worries I just have to ask for something and I get it because they want to make up for them breaking up our family.

I can stay up, out or leave when ever I want. But since my friends still have to be home just like I used to have to be so there isn't anyone to hang with. It was fun at first. I even went through every drawer and cabinet in the house. As long as I answer my cell and give the right answers and clean up anything I have been into I can eat, drink or smoke anything I want and no one even knows.

Its easy to be around the little bit of time they want to see me. Then I have to stand there and listen to each parent tell everyone what a good kid I am and how well I am handling the divorce.

They don't seem any better off than before and it's really all a waste. I hate them for not caring and just keep thinking what fools they are.

Austin M.

Children's Letters to the Judge

187. Dear Judge,

We still haven't heard from Paul and don't know where he is. Mom has settled down since we found some places on the internet to leave messages for him.

Dad stops buy and picks me up for dinner every Friday night. We have dinner and talk.

The after school job at mom's company has turned into full time until summer is over. Most of our classes are filled with adults who need to learn business programs to get a better job and I like helping them.

It's not the family we had but it is the family we have now and we are doing the best we can.

Kelton

188. Dear Judge,

I told you this divorce would never work. We are all back living in the house again.

Seth

Children's Letters to the Judge

189. Dear Judge,

I was 6 when you awarded custody to my mother, my father took me away, saying, it would be the only way we could be together and happy. With the re-tellings, and explanations, I thought I was part of decision to leave.

Drama in our lives was intense with plots of those attempting to hunt us down and harm us. Everyone on a motorcycle was part of my mother's boyfriend's gang. Police officers were on the take and working for my mother. She ruined every chance we had by sending bad guys after us. We lived shadow lives for seven years changing our names every time we moved. Living in pay-by-the-week motels, I watched TV days while my father slept. Then we did reading, writing and math lessons and worked nights. My father was arrested when the police investigated a fight he got into at work and he told them where to find me.

I am living with my mother and it is strained. I am angry that my father taught me that my mother was dangerous. I still don't trust her even thought I know she isn't who my father said she was. I feel like a bad daughter for hiding from my mother and for betraying my father by learning to love my mother. We didn't have a life when we were running. I want this, but it is hard. I want a life with my mother and her husband an my half sisters. I want a pet. I want to go to school. Most of all I want to belong.

I hope you won't put my father in jail. It isn't what my mother or I want. Everyone makes mistakes.

Have a wonderful day, Tara

Dear Judge,

190. Dear Judge,

Please have the valuator come back out to our house. The day she came was not a day like all the rest. The kitchen caught fire because my brother was trying to make cheese grill sandwiches for us kids to eat so mom could talk to the valuator. Tell Miss Hill the dog never peed on anyone before and we will put him outside this time.

Yours truly,

Bobby J.

Children's Letters to the Judge

Current Titles

Witness Guide
For any kind of case.
ISBN 1-58747-066-7
by Charlotte Hardwick

Killers & Boosters
Attitude adjustment for child custody litigants.
ISBN 1-58747-043-8
Compiled by Charlotte Hardwick

Case Management Forms
For Child Custody Battles.
ISBN 1-58747-069-1
Compiled by Charlotte Hardwick

Win Your Child Custody War
12th Edition
ISBN: 1-58747-071-3
by Charlotte Hardwick

Dear Judge,

New Books for 2009 - 2010

Parenting at a Distance
When the children you hold in your heart live someplace else.
ISBN 1-58747-008-X
by Charlotte Hardwick

Video for Child Custody Cases
Visually telling your story.
ISBN 1-58747-072-1
by Charlotte Hardwick

Supervised Visitation During Child Custody Battles
A book for parents dealing with court-ordered supervision.
ISBN 1-58747-073-X
by Charlotte Hardwick

Evidence for Child Custody Cases
How to document your child custody case.
ISBN 1-58747-074-8
by Charlotte Hardwick